on track ...

Roy Harper

every album, every song

Opher Goodwin

sonicbondpublishing.com

Sonicbond Publishing Limited
www.sonicbondpublishing.co.uk
Email: info@sonicbondpublishing.co.uk

First Published in the United Kingdom 2021
First Published in the United States 2021

British Library Cataloguing in Publication Data:
A Catalogue record for this book is available from the British Library

Copyright Opher Goodwin 2021

ISBN 978-1-78952-130-6

Typeset in ITC Garamond & ITC Avant Garde
Printed and bound in England

Graphic design and typesetting: Full Moon Media

on track ...
Roy Harper

every album, every song

Opher Goodwin

Acknowledgements
With thanks to Liz Goodwin and Mark Ruston for their help.

on track ...

Roy Harper

Contents

Introduction

Roy Harper is a unique individual and an innovative songwriter who took his first uncharacteristically tentative steps into the London folk scene during the mid-1960s. He was born on 12 June 1941 into the middle of World War II, his mother sadly dying a few days later from mastitis: a common breast infection, nowadays easily treatable. The loss of his mother, naturally, had a lifelong impact on Roy's personality. His father married again, but his stepmother was a strict, religious woman, and Roy's life of rebellion began.

His first memory is of being held in someone's arms, looking towards a red glow on the horizon, and being told, 'Manchester's really copping it tonight'. As a wayward child, his younger years were marked by constant trouble, both at home and school. On one occasion, he was found many miles from home, pedalling his trike towards Liverpool. His dislike of the religion his stepmother imposed, led to him performing pagan ceremonies and burying effigies in his back garden.

As a child, Harper lived in the genteel town of Lytham St Annes: a place he once described as a cemetery with a bus stop. The tedium of life in the drowsy town portrayed a conservative ethos he fought against. Moving into his teenage years, minor incidents progressed into more serious crimes. He and a small group of friends alternated between running free in the countryside and conducting shoplifting and vandalism sprees. These activities ranged from stealing chocolates in Woolworths to breaking into Lytham's cricket pavilion. They drank the booze they found inside, then burnt the building to the ground.

On one occasion, Roy and a friend rampaged through the town, pulling up freshly planted roadside saplings, then hoisting a weighing machine through the public toilets' window. Exhausted, they searched for somewhere to put their heads down and broke into a garage. Falling asleep in a car, they were discovered the following morning: by the owner, who, unfortunately, happened to be a policeman.

Continued rebellion and a string of minor offences culminated in Roy's arrest. He was found guilty of daubing swastikas and a hammer and sickle on the town hall – the act ostensibly a protest aimed at the councillors (who he considered to be a bunch of Nazis) and against the Russian invasion of Hungary. It was sufficient to produce a double-spread article with photos in the Daily Mirror.

This was just the beginning.

At fifteen – in order to escape from his stepmother and the mayhem he had created – Roy signed up to the Royal Air Force for five years, with dreams of becoming a pilot. But life in the RAF was not how he imagined. He tried boxing, which provided some respite, but the unremitting discipline and tedium of life as a serviceman became unbearable. After two years, he knew he had to get out. Without the cash to buy his discharge, Roy decided to feign madness – not too difficult a task in his case. He successfully convinced the military doctors, and the RAF discharged him, but only as far as RAF Princess Mary's mental institution, where he was assessed and treated. There being sectioned, he was forcibly medicated with lithium and largactyl, and even subjected to electric shock therapy. Eventually transferred to Lancaster Moor Hospital, Roy decided that in order to keep his 'insanity', he had to escape. Being of slight build, he was able to squeeze through a fanlight window and flee. I have a mental image of him, wearing one of those gowns that tie at the back, racing across the grass and scaling the wall – although I'm sure it probably wasn't quite like that.

Now on the run, Roy headed for Blackpool, where he became immersed in the bohemian subculture. As a self-proclaimed hashish-smoking beatnik, he discovered the world of Kerouac, Ginsberg, and Burroughs and began to write poetry.

However, he continued with his reckless ways. Undeterred by the risk of being caught and sent back to the institution, Roy resumed his rampage through life. On one evening – at a party that was running out of booze – he climbed onto shop roofs, intending to break into an off-licence. Crashing through a skylight, he found himself miraculously unscathed but on the floor of a chemist. Unable to open the dangerous drugs cupboard, he settled for a bottle of amphetamines and a jar of pennies, proceeding to sit on the seashore, swallowing a handful of the pills and throwing pennies into the water.

Prone to falling in love easily and heavily, Roy's teenage years were marked by two serious love affairs. Unfortunately, both girls became pregnant, were forced to have abortions, and prevented from having further contact with Roy.

Beginning to write beat poetry, and after walking the streets of Blackpool reciting poetry for a full 24 hours ending with a recital on the pier, he gained prominence in Blackpool's Evening Gazette as the Marathon Jazz Poet. A 1960 poetry reading in Newcastle was his first paid gig.

Following his and his two brothers' brief attempt at a skiffle group – De Boys – Roy headed for the continent, hitchhiking and busking his way around, playing standard country-blues numbers. His first gigs with seated audiences were in Danish folk clubs in 1961.

Returning from his European adventures, he went to London, where his wild ways continued. After being hauled down from the King's Cross Station roof, he was arrested once more. Convicted of a number of offences, he was detained at Her Majesty's pleasure. This short, sharp shock left a lasting impression.

Upon his release, Roy set off for the continent again, this time with Mocy, soon to become his first wife. While Roy busked, Mocy made a more lucrative income from her street art: chalk copy drawings of major artworks. Returning to London in the mid-1960s, they rented a flat in Kilburn, married, and had a child: Nick. Needing a steady income – but with a conventional job being unsuited to his exuberant character – Roy had the idea of combining his poetry with music and attempted to break into the music business. Music and poetry probably saved him from what could have been a very troubled life. The sometimes exciting but often tragic experiences of those wild years shaped Roy's life and personality, becoming the stimuli for much of his songwriting.

Peter Bellamy of the 1960s folk group, The Young Tradition, befriended Roy, encouraging him to go down the route of traditional folk music. But Roy had other ideas. Peter introduced him to Andy Matheou, who ran a basement club called Les Cousins on Greek Street in Soho – the club the centre of London's burgeoning contemporary folk scene. Andy gave Roy a slot, and he soon became a regular performer and headline act with a loyal following.

Surrounded by the very best of British acoustic guitar talent, Roy, instead of following the traditional folk/blues route, began melding his love of jazz and beat poetry with contemporary folk guitar. His friends and inspirations were Davy Graham, Bert Jansch, John Renbourn and Jackson C. Frank. He also knew Al Stewart, Whiz Jones, John Martyn and Paul Simon. They were all copying and competing with each other.

In those early years, Roy's life was one long party: sitting around with musicians, playing, talking, smoking and developing his music. By 1965, he'd created his own unique, distinctive and experimental style. Because of the acoustic nature of his performances, he was playing the folk clubs, including his regular spot at Les Cousins. But Roy was eager to take it further. At some point, Joe Lustig became his manager and secured him a dubious record deal.

In 1967, when I first saw Roy perform in Les Cousins, I was hooked. Soon after that, I met him and we became friends. Roy was about to be unleashed onto an unsuspecting world. His first album was in the can, and he was working on more ambitious projects.

This book takes you on a journey through those extraordinary years, with all their ups and downs. I include personal memories and descriptions of every album and track that Roy has released.

Sophisticated Beggar (1966)

First released on the Strike label in 1966
Personnel:
Peter Richards: producer
Roy Harper: guitars, vocals and all songwriting
Paul Brett: guitar
Bert Jansch: guitar
John Rebourn: guitar
Richie Blackmore: electric guitar
Lon Goddard: guitar and the drawing for the cover.
Unknown: drums and organ

The title says it all. Roy saw himself as being outside of mainstream society. He used his intelligence and creativity to scrounge a living. He was and still is, the sophisticated beggar.

Pierre Tubbs produced this album for Strike Records. The story is that a bunch of shady underworld characters were laundering money, and they set up Strike in order to hide their activities. Roy claimed it to be a true garage album because it was recorded in a makeshift studio, converted from a potting shed in Leatherhead. As studios go, it was a primitive setup, and the album was recorded on a basic Revox tape machine. Out came this remarkable album, which is quite unlike anything his contemporaries had produced.

Nobody seems to remember exactly who played on what. No professional notes were made. The tape was left to roll, and the numbers were mainly single takes with a minimum of overdubs. The equipment wasn't up to much and options were limited. Only one or two tracks were worked on further and added to – notably the single and the other chosen as its B-side.

For the time, it is surprising and unusual that Roy didn't want to include any of the folk/blues songs he'd been busking with. All the songs are Roy Harper originals. Also surprising is the album showing such a range of style and complexity, coupled with poetic lyrics. Roy was already experimenting, adding jazz chords and even using rock backing. His vision was much wider than most other folk artists. Not only is the album more original in content than that of his contemporaries, but it's more ambitious and avant-garde. He knew what he wanted and was extending his musical prowess. He might have been playing folk clubs with an acoustic guitar, but this album clearly demonstrated that there was a lot more to Roy.

Sophisticated Beggar has been re-released a number of times (and was illegally bootlegged by Tring Records as *Legend*). It also appeared as *Return of the Sophisticated Beggar*, with the additional track, 'Hup Hup Spiral': which is simply Roy saying, 'Hup hup hup', as the stylus moves to the disc centre and lifts.

'China Girl'

The opening track of Roy's career is remarkable. People expecting some type of folk song were about to be amazed. This song is much rockier than they would've expected – not Roy with a guitar, but Roy with a whole band.

This was only 1966 but listen to that phasing as Roy makes the music into a psychedelic masterpiece. This was the very dawn of psychedelia, and Roy was riding it.

The song was written about a beautiful Chinese girl he used to see in Soho. The lyric's willow patterns, dragons and sunsets, create a magical landscape. It is an example of the way Roy was merging his poems with music.

The track set the tone for the rest of the album.

'Goldfish'

In contrast to 'China Girl', 'Goldfish' has a catchy tune and is a much simpler acoustic number. It starts with a basic melody plucked out on guitar, the vocal then mirroring it – the song changes at the chorus, with the backing growing in symphonic effect.

Written for Roy's baby son Nick, 'Goldfish' is a fine example of a contemporary folk song. The deft poetic touch makes it much more than a lullaby. The second guitarist on this track is Lon Goddard.

'Sophisticated Beggar'

The busy title track features the duelling guitars of Roy and John Renbourn. Together they create a full sound that produces the power of a complete band.

The song enshrines Roy's antisocial attitude. He has no desire to be part of a society based on emptiness and greed. He does not aspire to fast cars, tinpot religions or the acquisition of wealth. He has something far more: a head full of ideas and vitality, and he's living life to the full.

'My Friend'

On this acoustic track, Roy demonstrates his finger-picking style, along with the use of harmonics. The song was written for Jackson C. Frank: a groundbreaking New York singer/songwriter who had a tragic past. He suffered horrendous burns in a school fire when a number of his friends were killed, including his girlfriend. Many years later, in 1964, after receiving a financial settlement, Jackson came to England on the Queen Elizabeth, with a Native American girlfriend. He is reputed to have written a superb set of songs on the journey, including 'Blues Run The Game'. But this is open to debate as many of the songs were possibly written previously.

Jackson rapidly assimilated into the Les Cousins folk scene, along with fellow American Paul Simon. Jackson's songwriting style had a profound impact on other musicians. He recorded only one album – simply titled *Jackson C. Frank*. Paul Simon produced it, with Al Stewart on second guitar. The album was a milestone for other folk singers and is now a classic.

Jackson and Roy became friends. They would hang out, getting stoned, laughing and pondering the meaning of life into the early morning hours. But Jackson was profligate with money and soon found himself penniless. Suffering stage fright and writer's block – and with his mental health deteriorating – he eventually returned to New York.

'My Friend' is a heartfelt farewell and reminiscence of Roy and Jackson's close relationship. The gold and silver of the lyric are the opening words of Jackson's 'Milk And Honey': a song about leaving.

Roy sings with a mellow sadness as he recounts the depth of their friendship and the laughter they shared. He embellishes his poetic lyrics, creating a melancholic, affectionate melody over a bed of intricate guitar notes.

'Big Fat Silver Aeroplane'

A song featuring acoustic guitars, more in keeping with Roy's live performances and the contemporary folk scene. The song's basic themes are social commentary and drugs. It relates directly to Roy's bohemian life as a busker, reflecting his observation of fat tourists flocking abroad on holiday without wanting to understand the cultures they find.

Yes, 'Turn again Whittington' (a reference to Dick Whittington, who of course believed the streets of London were paved with gold) – the pursuit of wealth is a pointless endeavour that rarely brings fulfilment or happiness.

Oblique drug references fill the song: the demon firework eater is a reference to acid; the pop-eyed rabbit medal sucker is purple hearts (amphetamine); the line about heads falling off is a reference to the way teeth fall out through speed overuse; and both 'turning the Sunday joint' and 'spliff me plenty' are cannabis references. Roy's poetic and intricate disguises layer the lyrics, which only a minority (at that time) would understand, and which he obviously greatly enjoyed playing too. He goes on to take a swipe at pseudo-spiritual seekers and society in general, with polystyrene obelisks representing a plastic culture within which people are not living but breathing.

Roy called this a pop song. It is a vivid example of how his successful marriage of poetry and music expressed his anti-establishment sentiments at the beginning of the 1960s youth culture. Not really a pop song.

'Blackpool'

Davey Graham – a good friend and musician that Roy greatly admired – set the standard for instrumentals like this with his wonderful song, 'Anji'. At Les Cousins in the mid-1960s, the acoustic guitarist's had a friendly rivalry. They studied each other's tunings, chords and finger-picking styles – 'borrowed' and tried to outdo each other.

Even at this early stage, you could see that Roy was unusually talented. This was one of the first songs I ever saw him play. Sandwiched between Bert Jansch and John Renbourn (both of whose brilliance I was already familiar with) at

Les Cousins, Roy performed 'Blackpool', 'Goldfish' and one other, which might have been 'My Friend'. I was now mesmerised by the faultless skill of Roy's finger-picking and his originality.

The one line of lyric harks back to his youthful Blackpool days, and to the night he broke into an off-licence, crashed through the skylight of a chemist shop, and left through the front door, clutching a jar of amphetamines and another of pennies. Here Roy is thinking back to the beach where he was throwing handfuls of pennies into the sea and remembering them plinking into the water like raindrops.

'Legend'

This is another busy song with intricate guitars. I think Bert Jansch is on second guitar. With Bert Jansch, John Renbourn and Ritchie Blackmore all featuring on this first album, we can see that right from the start, Roy was working with the very best musicians. The guitars certainly create a driving sound, which, along with the biting lyrics, make this one of the album's strongest songs.

The poem is a savage attack on society – 'The sea of living dead stranded in amorphous tastelessness. 'The hollow men' is a reference to T. S. Eliot's poem of the same name. The line alluding to knowing 'the way to Mount Street' comes from Roy's time in prison. There was a Billy Bunter type in jail with him: a middle class, well-to-do chap, imprisoned for fraud. Mount Street is the finance centre of London, and this man once said to Roy, 'I know the way to Mount Street'.

To the fore, here is Roy's interest in history and that it merely records the exploits of the powerful, the robber barons – 'Landmarks in the desert wastes of multi-coloured crime'. This is a reworking of Jean Jacques Rousseau's thoughts – a philosopher Roy was smitten with. There is conjecture as to whether Roy is singing 'The false teeth in the cologne partly sharing half the load' or 'The false teeth in the colon'. I think it is the colon, and he is referring to everyone talking out of their backsides. Knowing Roy, he probably wanted both allusions.

Roy's answer to this pointless roadmap to nowhere is to take some amphetamine because it's an infinite universe out there that has no meaning: 'Everything is just everything because everything just is'.

It's an extremely powerful poem, packed full of meaning and set to music. The lyric was later rewritten with completely different subject matter and minor musical modification to become 'Referendum' on his 1975 album, *HQ*.

'Girlie'

This track also features two acoustic guitars. They create a flowing, intricate backing – much lighter than on the previous number – over which Roy delivers a poetic lyric: a eulogy to a pretty girl. It sounds very much like the style of Bert Jansch to me. Roy says this song was inspired by a picture of a girl on his wall. He would get ripped and dance in front of her – a very incongruous image.

'October The Twelfth'

A doleful number, with Lon Goddard on second guitar. It's a subdued dirge-like song that speeds up as it progresses but never breaks its initial mode of mournful depression. Roy's voice wails in a desultory low key.

He describes this as a bad day. Through a series of venomous questions on the pointlessness of life, meaningless existences, lies, falsehoods and the prop of religion, he hits out at society, then turning it back upon himself: 'It's me that's all wrong'.

'Black Clouds'

This features Roy and guitar in another Jansch-style number. It's played on an authentic Spanish guitar, bought for £12 in Figuras, Northern Spain – a guitar that adds a pleasant ringing sound as Roy picks his way through the complicated backing. The song is about a love that looks doomed. The clouds are gathering. Will she be there tomorrow?

'Mr. Station Master'

I don't know who played the organ on this track, but they created a totally different feel; a kind of fairground psychedelia. This is one of the full-band numbers, with guitars kept in the background. Roy's delivery sounds controlled as he fits in with the other musicians.

This humorous track was much needed to lift the atmosphere of the previous two numbers. Roy has a series of these entertaining songs that he brings out in his live act to lighten the mood. He calls them his 'best George Formby'.

When he wasn't hitching to gigs, Roy would travel by train. That meant endless waiting on icy platforms, freezing to death and blaming the stationmaster for poor service; so cold, he was contemplating suicide and dreaming up comic lyrics to take his mind off his frozen feet.

'Forever'

Forever is played on guitar with steel strings and features the use of harmonics. Roy's voice is passionate, sincere and gentle, enhancing the melody of one of the most beautiful love songs ever written. It was written for Mocy, his first wife. The poem is about the contentment of lying next to the one you love in the early dawn, watching her sleep, and contemplating slipping through time together. It is openly romantic, sentimental and delightful. Roy often played the song in his live act and liked it so much that he re-recorded it for his 1974 *Valentine* album.

'Committed'

'Committed' is quite a contrast – a mad rollicking full-band electric romp – and the kind of rock freak-out that is a million miles away from the acoustic and gentle 'Forever'. It is loud, uproarious, and a great album finale. But it falls to pieces at the end, as Roy forgets the lyrics and ad-libs through maniacal laughter, which is quite apt for the song's subject matter. I have never heard him perform this track live, and the forgotten lyrics have been forever lost, so we will never know what they were.

'Committed' is about his stay in a mental hospital after feigning madness so as to be released from the RAF when he was seventeen. The song gaily lists the horrific treatments on offer, from ECT through to padded cells and lobotomy, as psychiatry attempts to tame the wildness and subdue the spirit. Roy was forcibly subjected to a number of these (padded cells, largactyl, lithium and ECT) to help him fit into the 'monotony' of society.

Outtakes
These outtakes were demos recorded on a mono Ferrograph quarter-inch tape machine. After regaining the song rights and retrieving the original tapes from Pierre Tubbs, they were eventually released on the Science Friction CD, *Today Is Yesterday*, in 2002.

'Long Hot Summer's Day'
Roy's acoustic guitar (which he chose to fit with nylon strings) creates a mesmerising melody, on which he hangs his poetry about young love. A hot summer day sitting around, talking and flirting. Perhaps not his strongest song, but it could have worked on the album.

'The Scaffold Of The Daylight'
An unassuming song, based around an intricate, finger-picked melody. It is a hash song from Roy's stoned days spent busking. Free as a bird – 'Just a billionaire well-disguised as a peasant'.

'In The Morning'
A simple arrangement based around some crisp finger-picking, using nylon strings again. This is a love song; a poem about a young man wandering through empty streets, long after dark, when everyone else is in bed. He is thinking about his young lady, wanting to show her the beauty in nature all around and protect her from the horror of mankind.

'Love'
Another acoustic number with a second guitar, probably played by Bert Jansch. The song is a little downbeat for a eulogy to love and sounds rather Janschian in delivery.

Roy has always been in love with love. He relishes the euphoria of those early months in a relationship. This craving for love has fuelled many a song, and this was one of the first. He wants that endorphin rush to last forever. He runs through a series of metaphors: likening love to cherry stones, laughing children, crazy dreams and mountain streams. As Roy says: 'An age of burning stories that never can be told'.

17

'Little Old Lady'

This is yet another song demonstrating Roy's adept finger-picking, with some additional trills thrown into the mix. He is contemplating old age and thinking about how an old lady's dreams changed as her world became limited by age and also by the strictures of a greedy society. Roy is young, and it's his turn to live and chase his dreams. The lyric offers an interesting perspective, but it doesn't quite work and is a little strange.

'Mountain'

This has quite a forceful introduction for what is essentially a love song. Roy certainly gives it some welly as he belts out words and demonstrates his vocal purity and power.

This was one of his first love songs. He said he was going for the operatic, and it certainly feels like that. The mountain: a metaphor for the size of their love? Their minds? Their lives? Perhaps all of them? Who knows?

Unreleased Tracks

It's hard to understand why these tracks were not included (along with the single) on an extended version of the first album. Putting some of them out on *Today Is Yesterday* – along with an assortment of diverse early obscure singles and outtakes from other albums – produced a mishmash that doesn't really work for me. I could not really understand why the four other tracks were left off. A couple of them were equally as good as those that were included.

'It's A Long Promised Land'

This track features Roy on his nylon-stringed acoustic, demonstrating his distinctive picking. It is a song of some merit. It takes a swipe at the unfulfilled promise of both religion and politics.

'Deal Me In'

This sounds like an attempt to create a pop single, and so was given the full band treatment; drums and electric guitar. The song is not at all Harper-like; in fact, the lyrics are trivial. The vocal sounds out of key, but that might just be the tape version I have. I can see why Roy did not include this on the album.

'Much More Than That'

Strummed on acoustic guitar in much the same mode as 'Deal Me In', this was another attempt at producing a single that was probably abandoned at an early stage because it didn't work. Roy was not good at producing pop songs at the request of record companies. This is a throwaway song without substance.

'Can't You Hear Me (Puppet Show)'

This started as a poem called 'Puppet Show': an early example of Roy's beat poetry. The recording is not of the best quality, being a bit muffled, which might be why it wasn't included on Today is Yesterday. But the mystery is, why wasn't it professionally recorded for inclusion on *Sophisticated Beggar?* It certainly had real potential.

The lyric is a dense poem, with Roy railing against society and the whole puppet show of the universe again. Full of wonderful imagery, the song has a great chorus – the lyric from the perspective of a destitute, penniless itinerant musician. An excellent song.

Single
'Take Me Into Your Eyes'
The track that was finally selected and worked on was written as a pop track. Roy has said that it was recorded in the hopes of paying a month's rent.

Right from the first notes, you can tell this was a single aimed at the charts: complete with a full band consisting of drums, electric guitar, bass and effects. Featuring the guitar of Ritchie Blackmore (very much to the fore), it is a catchy number with a brief chorus of backing singers, with a psychedelic style similar to the later Yardbirds. Being quite commercial, it could have caught on, but didn't. Maybe it was this single that gave the CBS label the idea that they could make Roy into an (unlikely) pop star.

'Pretty Baby' (B-Side)
An upbeat number with a full band sound, including tambourine! The production is unlike the rest of the album and it was specifically recorded as the single B-side, so was given the full-band treatment.

It's another song much in the style and delivery of Bert Jansch, and that is probably Bert playing alongside Roy. The two were good friends, and Roy had helped Bert out by playing second guitar on a couple of numbers from his second album, *It Don't Bother Me*: Roy sang and played guitar on 'A Man I'd Rather Be', and played guitar on 'My Lover'.

The song is about a girl with whom Roy used to have 'noisy sex', but she left him for somebody else: maybe Bert Jansch?

Come Out Fighting Ghengis Smith (1967)

First released on the CBS label in 1967
Personnel:
Shel Talmy: producer
Roy Harper: guitar and various instruments. Writer of all the songs
Laurie Allan: drums
Keith Mansfield: strings
Bert Jansch: liner notes
Lippa Pearce: cover design

A second album is often difficult. Musicians perfect the songs they use in their live act and select the best for their first album. When it comes to the second, they are often short of good material. However, that was not the case for Roy. Far from running short of ideas, his second album teems with new concepts and strong songs. It even features Roy's first long epic: 'Circle'.

Perhaps CBS had heard something in Roy's Strike recordings and heard about his live performances, or perhaps his manager – Joe Lustig – just talked a good talk. Either way, they decided that Roy was worth taking a punt on. Hoping that he would come up with chart material, they brought in American producer Shel Talmy, who had previously worked with The Who and The Kinks, amongst others, and was really an expert at creating singles. Singles were not what Roy was about: he was an album singer-songwriter who mainly worked acoustically. Roy and Shel were not the ideal combination. In an interview with the magazine, Musoscribe, Shel described working with Roy: 'Roy Harper was difficult. The word that comes to mind is … truculent'. Talmy didn't deny Harper's talent, but the two men's approaches were at odds: 'Whenever I record anybody, I generally have a little chat: 'Do you guys want to sell records, or do you just want to sit there and wank in the dark or something?'. Talmy said that he liked making records that would sell and that when making *Come Out Fighting Ghengis Smith*, Harper 'probably wasn't particularly interested (in that), and we battled. But we got 'round to it'.

I can well imagine. Roy does not do compromise. He knows what he wants, and it's all about artistic integrity. He's not interested in producing hit singles and wants to produce good music. Even so, somehow, the pair formed a working relationship that resulted in a superb album. *Come Out Fighting Ghengis Smith* was released in 1967, along with two singles, neither of which had The Beatles at all worried.

In 1991, the album was re-released on Andy Ware's Awareness Records, in an expanded form containing a strange assortment of bonus tracks, all of which will be reviewed later with the appropriate albums. These were 'Zaney Janey': an outtake from *Folkjokeopus,* that appeared on the American album along with 'Ballad Of Songwriter', in place of the instrumental, 'One For All'; the single, 'Midspring Dithering', and its B-side 'Zengem'; the outtake from *Flat Baroque and Berserk*, 'It's Tomorrow And Today Is Yesterday'; and two songs from the BBC radio show, Top Gear, in 1969: 'Francesca' and 'She's The One'.

Come Out Fighting Ghengis Smith, whilst perhaps being no better an album than its predecessor, is certainly a step forward musically. It's experimental, adventurous and avant-garde. There are spoken-word sections and a poem: not the usual thing for a rock/folk album. No wonder Shel Talmy found working with Roy difficult. CBS also found the experience mind-blowing. It was not quite the chart-friendly album they had envisaged. Roy said they did not know what to make of it.

The album is highly original and personal, with the epic, 'Circle', focussing on Roy's childhood. But the fact that the album didn't easily slot into any particular genre is a dilemma that has constantly hounded Roy. The use of strings, a low-key backing and Roy's acoustic guitar take it into new territory. It certainly isn't folk or folk rock: it's Roy Harper. Yet Roy did not like the album, calling it the skeleton in his cupboard, even though it was ground-breaking in so many novel and experimental ways. I cannot think of another album from that period that has poems, spoken-word sections, or this type of poetic song. It was special, and different to the normal folk/blues or even Bob Dylan's then-current contemporary style. The album is uniquely English in style and composition. Its orchestral and pastoral atmosphere brings to mind Nick Drake's first two albums, though it predates them by a few years. They all have a similar willowy feel.

Bert Jansch wrote the weird cover notes, along with two little poems of dubious relevance to either Roy or the album.

The idea was for the song titles to be read as a continuum instead of a list. It almost works.

'Freak Street'

The opening track sets the tone for the album. The production is different from the debut. The addition of strings (unusual for that time) has a muting effect on the guitars, pushing them back in the mix. Laid-back snare drum creates a jazz feel that carries the track along. Although it makes for a muddy sound (much clearer on the remaster), I like the effect. The vocal is clear and melds well with the backing – Roy giving vent to his full vocal range.

The poem/lyric is complex, with much use of alliteration. It dictates the track's tempo, which speeds up and slows down in keeping with the words, which at times come thick and fast (making them difficult to decipher), and at others, slower, and thus more easily understood. The result is a beautiful song, teeming with poetic descriptions and expressively delivered.

Greek Street is in the centre of London's Soho – where the freaks and buskers hung out – and Roy renamed it Freak Street. An area that was once grand was now a place of dives, sex shows and cosmopolitan bohemia; a place where it all happened: dope, sex, caked-on make-up, Newcastle brown and music, in 'a neon desert storm of tin can shabbiness'.

A powerful start to the album.

'You Don't Need Money'

This track represented the album on the CBS sampler *The Rock Machine Turns You On* – where it was retitled as 'Nobody's Got Any Money In The Summer' – and was also the B-side of the single, 'Life Goes By'. I'm not sure it was the wisest choice for the sampler. 'Freak Street' would have portrayed Roy in a more serious mode.

'You Don't Need Money' is one of Roy's 'George Formby's' – a humorous song that always went down well at gigs: particularly the line about the 'Chinese wrestler's jockstrap cooked in chip fat'. The less lavish production suits it: Roy and his doubled-tracked guitar, with drums, work well.

It's a simple tale of a poor starving busker whose student audience belted off for the summer months to go hitch-hiking around the world, leaving him destitute. But then, who needs money? 'Except, of course, for scoring on a sunny day'.

'Ageing Raver'

With the third track, we are back to the full band. Shel gave it an upbeat production, with guitars, tambourine, bass, drums and strings. He was really trying his best to create a commercial sound, and it pounds along with a very catchy chorus.

The lyric describes the life of a young London raver. Spliffed out of his head, he is lying about in the sun and busking to get by. Rich girls – beguiled by the decadence, acid and speed – dip into the scene of all-night partying. Life is one long party. But then, already, before he's even grown up, is he getting too old for the part he is playing? At only 25, was Roy feeling his age?

'In A Beautiful Rambling Mess'

A gentle song in which sweeping strings and harpsichord create a wistful, ethereal quality, augmenting Roy's guitar.

The poem captures the moment of a sunset reverie. He describes himself sitting, watching the orange/red glow of the fires of the setting sun, and allowing it to set his mind adrift, roaming through memories, experiences and relationships, as time floats slowly past. 'What a beautiful rambling mess we live'.

'All You Need Is'

This gentle song starts with carefully picked guitar. The backing opens on a soft snare rhythm, with bass and keyboards in the background. The strings build and ebb, augmenting and emphasising the melody as Roy's voice rises and falls, culminating in his full falsetto.

The song comprises two parts. I used to mistakenly think the long first section related to an acid trip, but Roy denied that acid was involved. It was just one of those very emotional, introspective conversations. Roy is in deep discussion with his girlfriend about the nature of womanhood, sexuality, and her despair at her unequal, empty-headed, subservient role. He tells her it doesn't have to be that way: she can be free to live the life she wants.

The second section brings a change of mood, focussing on women in general, Roy delivering his comments in a direct and disdainful manner. The song then drifts into a repetition of 'All you need is', with a variety of emphasis. Is it a reaction to The Beatles' 'All You Need Is Love', from around the same time?

'What You Have'

Roy and acoustic guitars here create a haunting love song. The guitars interact in the background as Roy sings tenderly.

Verse one celebrates three years of time with his first wife Mocy, as well as describing the forces that tried to pull them apart. The telling word for me is the 'had' in the verse's seventh line. Verse two refers to a one-night stand with a girl called Summer, perhaps suggesting that Mocy tolerated an open relationship. Verse three is almost an apology, and the last verse is more enigmatic.

While this is a love song, it has a thoughtful sadness, as if Roy is mourning the waning of a great love. Sometimes, all you need is what you have.

'Circle'

'Circle' is the first of Roy's epics and is certainly not one that Shel could turn into a commercial success. It lasts over ten minutes and has five sections, including a spoken part: absolutely unique for its time. Each section employs different tempos and instrumentation. The song is the album's central point.

The piece starts with acoustic guitar strummed to a subdued drum rhythm. Then follows a spoken-word section – a strained conversation between Roy and his dad – over the sound of traffic. This leads to a faster sequence, featuring drums and bass, then subsiding into a slower, more intense part, with strings and drums in the background. The intense mood builds strongly through fast-plucking guitar, drums and strings, followed by a softer section in which Roy's voice rises to a falsetto at the end of each line. The strings appear again as the finale is reached.

It's an ambitious and exacting piece of work that must have tested both Shel and Roy in its creating – I can only imagine the conversations.

The lyrics deal with the constant childhood pressure on Roy to succeed – success being measured in wealth. His father is addressing Roy' accomplishments, and Roy is responding. The lyric moves from his rejection of religion to his adolescent striving for importance and acceptance towards the realisation that the only thing he can be, is himself. The song covers relationship betrayals and the inability to find answers. Roy's final assertion is that all we can do is live our lives.

The final spoken words are his Dad's, who – ironically, not understanding a word of the long introspection – says, 'Aye Lad – but I always knew you had it in you'.

'Highgate Cemetery'

One of Roy's experimental tracks, on which he sings a cappella. The reverb effect was produced by singing into the guitar soundhole while holding the strings in an open D chord. Performed live, it had quite an effect on the audience. The voice's ethereal ring seems appropriate, given the poem's subject matter is death. Roy uses the 'All You Need Is' technique of holding back the next word in order to create another meaning: 'It's a very rare feeling to be mindless and seeing... nothing', 'All you need is all... you need... is all... you need... is'. Extremely effective.

The song describes the strange feeling of being dead and buried (in Highgate Cemetery along with the Karl Marx tomb) and feeling nothing.

'Come Out Fighting Ghengis Smith'

Another epic, at over nine minutes. This track created controversy over Roy's assertion that he did not want wealth or fame. I always think this song/poem is really two separate pieces: the first part really not 'Ghengis Smith' at all. It's an unnamed song, with the poem, 'Come Out Fighting Ghengis Smith', attached to it.

The piece starts with double-tracked, acoustic guitars, Roy reciting the lyrics over them. When the catchy chorus kicks in, he sings, as the drums, keyboard and bass, spring up behind him, adding punch. Then we are back to the acoustic guitars and recitation. The second chorus has slightly different lyrics but the same musical oomph. After that, the song trails off into a spoken introduction to the poem.

The first section is a diatribe against God and society. Then follows a piece of false logic and tautology about the words 'inconceivable' and 'nothing', which is somewhat illogical but nevertheless thought-provoking. The lyric continues to suggest that if God existed, he would be in everything, including the mud that smothered the children in Aberfan (In October 1966, a mudslide from a coal tip, engulfed a local primary school, causing the death of 116 children and 28 adults).

The chorus is a whimsical, positive spin on regeneration. Verse two is about adopting a positive philosophy of life and just being yourself. Roy vehemently states that he doesn't want wealth or fame, which was controversial at the time, critics picking it up on numerous occasions. After a slightly altered chorus, Auntie Sally asks Roy what the hell he is doing, and the song trails off.

In the poem's short introduction, Roy talks to Jack. Jack, is Jack Kerouac (author of the classic Beat novel, *On The Road*). Then follows an anti-war poem, performed with a number of humorous voices, ending with a reference back to Aberfan.

Singles

CBS released two singles, including one track from the album.

'Midspring Dithering'

This is a frivolous pop song, totally different to the album's content. Actually, it is very chart-friendly, through being given the pop treatment with a full band, strings and brass – though, unfortunately, it didn't trouble the top 100. It's a bright, sparkly song about the joy of breaking out of the winter lockdown into the summer sunshine.

'Zengem'

This is the B-side of 'Midspring Dithering' – also given the full band treatment. I think it is more interesting than the A-side, as it has a jazz chord sequence and an injection of humour.

'Zengem' is a quaint, observational piece on life in Kilburn, London, where Roy was living. Every Sunday morning, the bells of the church across the road annoyingly woke him. This is a reflection on a strange society based purely on money, with no credence given to meaning.

'Life Goes By'

Roy here makes another attempt at a pop song. It's a jolly little number featuring a full band, brass and a kazoo. It's quite fun as Roy gives a jovial commentary on an empty society that only values money and views the whole youth culture with great suspicion – give them a bath, a short back and sides and conscription. Meanwhile, life goes by. The B-side was the *Come Out Fighting Ghengis Smith* track, 'You Don't Need Money'.

25

Folkjokeopus (1969)

First released on the Liberty label in 1969
Personnel:
Shel Talmy: producer
Roy Harper: vocals, acoustic guitar, psaltery or 'Composer Of Life' and writer of all songs
Jane Scrivener: vocals
Russ: bass guitar
Nicky Hopkins: keyboards
Clem Cattini: drums, percussion
Ron Geesin: arrangements and variety of instruments
Woody Woodward: cover design
Ray Stevenson: photo

The CBS arrangement had turned sour, and Liberty Records offered Roy a deal. Considering his previous stormy relationship with Shel Talmy, the two were paired up again. There was quite a buzz about this at the time. Roy's popularity was growing, and he had a whole new act, incorporating some powerful songs, including 'She's The One', 'One For All' and the amazing 'McGoohan's Blues'. There was an air of expectation. The London underground was in full swing and had adopted Roy.

The process of recording *Folkjokeopus* was fraught from the beginning. Working with Shel was again proving to be difficult. Liberty had promised the earth but was failing to deliver, and Roy found it impossible to communicate with anyone there. He said, whenever he had a problem, he was ushered into a room and had to talk to a monolith.

The atmosphere soon became toxic.

Eventually, the recording process became little more than a series of first takes. What is remarkable is the standard achieved from those sessions: a testament to Roy's abilities and the quality of the songs. The frustrating thing was, the songs – particularly 'McGoohan's Blues' – had not reached the potential evident from their live performances; they could have been so much better produced. Imagine if 'McGoohan's Blues' had been recorded in Abbey Road Studios with state of the art equipment, produced by Peter Jenner, with John Leckie or any of the other quality engineers!

The album difficulties didn't end with the recording. The cover, too, became a problem. Roy envisaged it as a photo in a diamond shape, but Liberty rotated the image, rendering it as a standard square. After much wrangling, Roy had to fork out his own money to have it changed. Even then, the result was not exactly as he envisioned. The cover is not quite a diamond, but somewhere in-between that and a square.

Roy's short time at Liberty was to prove frustrating. After many delays, the *Folkjokeopus al*bum finally emerged. The Liberty executives thought that long instrumentals were unlikely to go down well in America, and so 'Ballad of

Songwriter' and 'Zaney Janey' replaced 'One For All' on the American album, released by World Pacific Records.

'Sgt. Sunshine'
The album starts with the band launching into the upbeat 'Sgt. Sunshine'. This sets a storming pace, Roy's voice soaring above in a near falsetto, singing 'Sunrise'. From its opening notes, the song has more of a rock feel than anything on the previous album. It is quite a band, particularly considering the presence of the great Nicky Hopkins on keyboards. The recording has a brighter, sparkier production than that on CBS. It seems to me that Shel was going for a more commercial sound.

Roy had always wanted to sing duets with women, and Jane Scrivener's clear voice made for the ideal foil. This was the first of many successful duets over the course of his career. He was always smitten with the female singers of The Incredible String Band. I think I detect their significant influence on this album.

'Sgt. Sunshine' would've made a great single if there had not been so many open drug references. The lyrics describe the time a police officer defiantly lit up a marijuana joint outside City Hall, protesting the draconian drug laws. Roy – an ardent cannabis advocate – immediately called the officer Sgt. Sunshine, and wrote this song about him.

There is an oblique reference to the TV series, The Prisoner, with mention of the village. The show had a lasting impact on Roy, and its influence would recur in 'McGoohan's Blues'.

The basic premise of 'Sgt. Sunshine', is that society has the wrong priorities. A life spent striving for money and fearing death is certainly no way to live.

The song also appeared on the sampler, Gutbucket.

'She's The One'
'She's The One' had become an important highlight in the live act. When I first heard this album, it was a shock to hear the song with full band treatment instead of as an acoustic solo. The stereo separates Roy's guitar from the backing. The drums, bass and piano, do drive the track forward, giving more energy, but I feel it has less impact than the live performance. The driving pace tends to give a hurried feel as if charging along at too much of a gallop.

Roy's voice – particularly on those high notes – is crystal clear – his strong falsetto adding an extra dimension.

'She's The One' would've made a brilliant single, were it not seven minutes long and including a number of sex and drug references. It's about Roy and Mocy's break-up. During this period, Roy had many late-night discussions with Andy Matheou, the owner of Les Cousins. Andy thought Roy was mad to break up with Mocy, and told him so. Roy wove their conversations into the lyrics.

Regardless of my preference for the live acoustic version, this recording is a tour de force.

'In The Time Of Water'

This track is an experimental piece that appears to be influenced by The Incredible String Band. The Indian sound came through the use of tabla and sitar, the only time Roy played the sitar on record. The tabla provided a pulsing visceral beat as the sitar plucked and twanged, the sound wandering back and forth, mirroring the vocal melody.

The lyric theme is the Aquarian age, complete with water sounds. The words paint a surreal picture of Hyde Park's Serpentine Lake, describing dead fish, icicles and nonsense verse in a Japanese-style kaon. All very weird and very 1960s.

'Composer Of Life'

Another humorous experiment. The song is a short poem sung in falsetto, with a hand-held psaltery as accompaniment. A recorder plays over the extended outro. I only saw Roy play this song once, at a free Hyde Park concert. He played the psaltery, held up close to the microphone.

'Composer Of Life' goes from the ridiculous to the sublime – a delightful unique poem.

'One For All'

A largely instrumental eight-minute guitar track, with just a few lyric lines, unadorned by any frills or backing, just as it was performed live. The tune passes through many phases, using a number of jazz chords, rhythms and complex plucking. Roy really demonstrates his guitar skills on this one. At times it sounds like there are ten guitars, even though he is playing alone.

Guitarist, Davey Graham, pioneered this type of instrumental. Acoustic guitarists vied with each other to produce compositions matching the skills evident on Davey's signature tune, 'Anji'. Roy was one of the best. 'One For All' – a further development from the first album's instrumental, 'Blackpool' – used to be a storming part of Roy's act.

The title really should be 'One For Al', as it is about Albert Ayler: the jazz tenor saxophonist who Roy greatly admired and befriended when busking in Copenhagen.

'Exercising Some Control'

A comical song opens side two. It's a full band number with great piano from Nicky Hopkins, capturing the content's zaniness and fun. It's about a dog called Some Control. Roy actually used to have a mad dog that jumped out of the window when excited: he might well have been the prompt for the song. The music captures the lolloping feel and comedy of the lyric and is a vehicle to produce a touch of slapstick. Roy makes fun of the judiciary and police in a comical court scenario.

'McGoohan's Blues'

The album's main event is this eighteen-minute epic. It has a mountain of verses and not a single word wasted. The song consists of two parts typical of the longer Roy Harper compositions.

He began by writing two distinct poems that he then developed into songs. This masterpiece was achieved by marrying the two together.

Roy plays and sings solo for the first part: an amazing twelve minutes in length. A short bridging verse takes him into the final section when the full band springs into action. For those who have heard Roy perform this live, it does feel that the last part of the studio version is a little too busy, as driving along at too fast a rate masks Roy's powerful delivery. This is frustrating for those of us who would like a perfect production of such an important piece of work.

The song was recorded in one live take. Consequently, there are one or two minor glitches, but 'McGoohan's Blues' remains an immaculate piece of work, the likes of which few songs have ever matched.

The poem's first part is based on Patrick McGoohan's TV series, *The Prisoner*. The iconic 1960s series lambasts a range of 20th-century institutions, from religion to the law. Through verse after verse, the song hits out at TV, pop music, game shows, conformity, rules, regulations, propaganda, manipulation and control, as an invisible elite herd us into mindless automatons. This list of things to rail against is as pertinent now as it was fifty-odd years ago. The drama's main theme is that all of us are prisoners in this crazy global society, whilst outside 'the village', there is the possibility of a more natural way of life.

The second part is more philosophical and deals with the metaphysical proposition that reality is nothing more than a dream. One could spend hours analysing the poem and extracting various meanings. As with all Roy's poetry, there are many layers and much to unpick.

As a song, I think it is unparalleled. Apart from maybe one or two of Roy's later epics, nothing comes close – not even Dylan's vitriolic 'It's Alright Ma, I'm Only Bleeding', which is the nearest comparison I can make.

Roy's standard of poetry and musicianship is incredible. He sings with gusto and remembers all the words (a feat in itself), delivering the song with aggression and passion. The rest of the album pales into insignificance. 'McGoohan's Blues' is the album's reason for being.

'Manana'

What could possibly follow 'McGoohan's Blues'? Something light; a complete change of mood and tone, and 'Manana' fit the bill. That meant the prior song was sandwiched between two humorous numbers. Nicky Hopkins' piano is the main ingredient in this full-band number, Roy's guitar almost lost in the mix.

'Manana' sprang from Roy's recent visit to the laid-back country of Cuba. Starting with 'marks for artistic interpretation' – which is certainly appropriate following the brilliance of 'McGoohan's Blues' – 'Manana' is a bit of nonsense that takes the piss out of modern culture and pop songs.

And so, while you are still absorbing 'McGoohan's...' hammer blows, the album ends on a light note, fading out with Roy and his young son Nick, giggling away while messing around in the studio. Ending with laughter was becoming a feature of Roy's albums.

Conclusion

If I were a Liberty executive or Shel Talmy, I would have been looking at this album's songs and wondering where the single was. 'Sgt. Sunshine' was the only real contender but was not likely to receive much airplay. Consequently, no single was released.

They had no idea, did they? Both Roy and the album were ahead of their time: literate, tuneful, psychedelic, non-conformist, progressive. They didn't fit 'pop' like The Kinks or early Pink Floyd. It was pointless to sell Roy in that way. In many respects, the 1960s were not kind to Roy; he was still finding his feet and the musical culture of the time didn't really suit him. That's strange, given that he seems such an archetypal 1960s figure.

Outtakes

The sessions yielded two outtakes: neither of any great importance. They replaced 'One For All' on the American pressing and did not see the light of day in England until they were bizarrely released on the album *Today Is Yesterday* in 2002.

'Zaney Janey'

This song rather embarrassed Roy. It was a song he wrote for Jane Scrivener. He wondered what on earth Jane had made of it. The track – with full band treatment and Nicky Hopkins on piano once again – achieves a type of psychedelic madness. It's a lively song with some fine falsetto singing, and if it wasn't for the stereotypical daft lyrics, this might have made a good single.

'Ballad Of Songwriter'

Another track that Roy later described as embarrassing, this time because he felt it was a humiliating advert for himself. It sounds as if this track was also being prepared as a single, as it has a commercial production style and is the only track from the album sessions to feature a brass section and strings. Despite the dire lyrics, Roy does deliver a great vocal, and guitar flourishes.

Overall, this is little more than a pop song with psychedelic overtones – but it's still a great song if you don't listen to the words!

Flat Baroque and Berserk (1970)

First released on the Harvest label in 1970
Personnel:
Roy Harper: vocals, acoustic guitar, electric guitar on Hell's Angels and all songwriting
Pete Jenner: producer
David Bedford: strings
Skaila Kanga: harp on 'Song Of The Ages'
Tony Visconti: recorder on 'Tom Tiddler's Ground'
Keith Emerson: keyboards on 'Hell's Angels'
Lee Jackson: bass guitar on 'Hell's Angels'
Brian Davison: drums on 'Hell's Angels'
Recorded at Abbey Road Studio
Lon Goddard: gatefold cover design
John McKenzie: photography
Highest UK chart place: 20

In the late 1960s, EMI became aware of the burgeoning underground scene. With Pink Floyd, they had a few fingers in the pie, but EMI wanted an opportunity to delve deeper into this potential market. The answer, in 1969, was to set up a subsidiary label to specialise in music from the underground scene. That was the label, Harvest. They signed Deep Purple, The Battered Ornaments, Syd Barrett, Robert Wyatt, Pink Floyd, Edgar Broughton and others.

By 1969, Roy was making quite a name for himself. Pete Jenner – who managed the early Pink Floyd – recommended Roy to EMI. Pete had been impressed with Roy's Hyde Park free festival performances, and after hearing his recorded material, thought Roy had the ability to do more. So he became one of the first Harvest signings. The beauty of the deal was that, for the first time, Roy had access to top-quality recording facilities (Abbey Road Studios where The Beatles recorded), unlimited studio time, a quality producer in Pete Jenner (they became good friends and cannabis buddies), and brilliant sound engineers in Phil McDonald and Neil Richmond.

Roy was a prolific songwriter, and in 1969, he entered the studio with a batch of songs surpassing anything he had created previously. With a bunch of friends to egg him on; a producer happy to collaborate on the entire process; all manner of rock cognoscenti dropping in to listen, comment and contribute, Roy was all set for a ground-breaking album – and that is what we were treated to with the magnificent *Flat Baroque And Berserk*.

Even the gatefold cover was brilliant. Designed by an old friend, Lon Goddard (with a photograph by John McKenzie), Roy looks resplendent in a psychedelic shirt and flat cap. Eyes shut, cig in mouth, he is reclining on a chaise longue, with a background of flock wallpaper and a tiger growling into his face!

'Don't You Grieve'

Right from the start, the recording has a crispness and immediacy. Roy strums with vigour, his acoustic guitar ringing loud and clear.

This fast driving number – full of energy and controversy – is an interesting choice for the first track. It was written in DADGAD tuning (the bottom E is tuned down to D, and the top two strings – B and E – are tuned down to A and D), giving the guitar a meaty, psychedelic, Indian tone. Davey Graham invented this tuning, and it's why Roy has two guitars on stage: one in normal tuning, the other in DADGAD.

'Don't You Grieve' is Roy (an avowed atheist) giving his alternative view of Judas Iscariot. The song's premise is that it was essential for Jesus to be betrayed. Jesus requested that Judas – out of friendship, not malice or greed – should do the deed. Far from being a traitor, Judas was a good friend.

The lyrics are written in the first person, giving the song more impact. The album is off to a cracking start.

'I Hate The White Man'

Just as 'McGoohan's Blues' was the *Folkjokeopus* centrepiece, 'I Hate The White Man' is the guts of *Flat Baroque And Berserk*. Like 'McGoohan's Blues' the song is an extremely powerful statement.

Roy was very much aware of the difficulty in generating the required passion when he recorded 'McGoohan's Blues' in an empty studio. He wanted 'I Hate The White Man' to be a live recording in front of his own audience, and at what better venue, than Les Cousins: the small, intimate club that became his second home when he was starting out. Amazingly, EMI agreed, and their mobile recording studio was set up in the club. That is incredible because we now have a recording of the entire show, which later surfaced as Live At Les Cousins.

The decision to leave the spoken preamble on the record was a dubious one. Roy always likes to talk about the lyrics and explain the ideas within his songs. He wants the inherent meaning to be understood. But once you have listened to the introduction a few times, it begins to pale. He knew that with a title like 'I Hate The White Man', it would be easy to mistake the subject matter, and he felt the lyrics required explanation. But perhaps that might've been best kept for the liner notes or the live album?

The song features only Roy and his guitar, yet he creates a full and complex piece of music. Here he has reverted to normal tuning. The chords are powerful, and the voice is clear and pure. As the piece progresses, the passion builds and builds until it storms along, with Roy hitting the strings with real venom.

The poem has nothing to do with skin colour. It is all about an attitude. It concerns the empty culture, hypocrisy and arrogance of western society and its violence, avarice and inherent racism. Roy detests the destructive nature of western values. His central premise is that this so-called civilisation took away a natural hunter-gatherer way of life and replaced it with concrete and shackles.

'The land of look and see' refers to America and Native Americans prior to the European's arrival.

Roy is here hankering after a simpler life, away from this plastic society of drunkenness, guns, tear gas and an unfulfilling lifestyle. He aims his fury at the establishment and the lust for power and wealth that not only creates war – enslaving us and taking away our freedoms – but destroys the planet in the process.

Roy envisions a tragic nuclear finale to our violent culture, which in the face of historical evidence, will inevitably perish. At the song's end, 'the shooting star has summoned death's dark angel from his night'.

A four or five-minute version of this song could've made a hard-hitting single! It should have been Roy's 'Working Class Hero'. 'I Hate The White Man' has similar chords and arrangement to Lennon's piece but is a far better song. Roy's first missed opportunity, I think.

'Feeling All The Saturday'
How does Roy follow a song like 'I Hate The White Man'? Easy. He changes the vibe by using humour and singing one of his comical numbers. He deployed this same trick after 'McGoohan's Blues'.

'Feeling All The Saturday' nearly didn't make the album at all. There was a debate as to whether it fit with the record's general atmosphere. They even discussed cutting the track into the actual cover cardboard so that the cover itself could be played on a turntable! That might have been fun, but the sound quality would have been poor. Fortunately, the track was included, and the delightful song works brilliantly in the album's flow. It needed a light interlude.

Once again, the simple format of just Roy and guitar was chosen and worked to great effect. Even in this comical song, Roy manages to squeeze in a dig against the leaning post of religion and also a dash of philosophy concerning the nature of reality. Roy despises our culture's shallowness.

Around this time, Roy boarded a twelve-hour flight to Los Angeles, clutching a 400-page book on the world's greatest philosophers. The deepest thoughts and ideas of mankind have always fascinated him.

'How Does It Feel'
Just Roy and his guitar. Where Shel Talmy threw in the kitchen sink, Pete and Roy went for a simpler approach yet still managed to produce that full-blooded sound. The complex strumming pattern with the set of low D-based chords gives it power, and Roy's voice soars, full of despair and angst.

I think this was a ground-breaking song and could've been the second killer single. The production is perfect and direct. The Abbey Road equipment was brilliant, and the quality as good as anything recorded nowadays.

'How Does It Feel' is another social commentary. The lyric tackles society's claustrophobia, its two-faced lifestyles, and the driving ambition that prevents us from living freely. With our 'god strapped to (our) wrist', we are screwed into our pigeonholes. Once we start thinking, we soon realise there is no escape. Some turn to drink, some to religion, and others just wither away. 'You might as well start to freewheel'.

'How Does It Feel' is right up there with Roy's other epics but was largely overlooked until its recent featuring in the TV series, *The Handmaid's Tale*. Then, people took notice, and Roy received well-deserved acclaim.

'Goodbye'

Side one concludes with this song of disillusionment. 'Goodbye' is a heartfelt farewell. Roy's stronger songs often received a furious reaction from critics and a fanatical section of society. He realised he could actually be shot for speaking so openly. At one time, he took a toy gun on stage as a kind of challenge.

Far from being free from working-life drudgery, singing his songs for a living kept Roy tied to the corporate showbiz machine, and he was feeling the pressure. Contemplating giving up, he wrote this tender song as his resignation letter.

His voice is full of feeling, the guitars crisp and sharp. There are beautiful harmonies and imagery. The words highlight the hypocrisy and avarice of the cut-throat showbiz world. Roy yearns for freedom and a carefree life – to spend time with the woman he loves. 'Goodbye' is a beautifully crafted letter of withdrawal from the rat race his life had become.

'Another Day'

Here is a mystery. Why was this track not considered as a single? Surely it would have been a hit, and possibly Roy's third killer single from this one album (following 'I Hate the Whiteman' and 'How Does It Feel').

'Another Day' is written in standard tuning, with a very telling C Major 7th chord to kick it off. Major 7ths are wistful, spacey chords, beloved of The Cocteau Twins, Roy's 'doppelganger' Roger Waters, and all manner of new age musicians. As Brian Eno said: 'I loathe the 'new age' because there's no menace in it'.

This is a love song of such aching intensity that it touches anyone who hears it. Roy's voice is perfect, warm and emotional, complete with a slight warble. His guitar subdued, augmenting a mood of great melancholy. It is the album's first track to feature strings: perfectly arranged by David Bedford. They help us imagine the sorrow and pathos of meeting with a past love: a meeting of unspoken longing.

Kate Bush, Peter Gabriel and This Mortal Coil recognized the song's quality and all later recorded it. Kate and Peter perform it as an excellent duet, which can be found on YouTube.

'Davey'

A delightful song played simply on guitar, using Roy's distinctive finger-picking technique.

Davey was Roy's younger brother. In his teens, Roy, Dave and their other brother Harry, formed a skiffle group called De Boys. This song is a tribute to Dave. Roy remembers the time when, as young lads, they went out on the sandbars of the Lancaster coast and became marooned, the incoming tide nearly drowning them. They had to wade through the fast-flowing current to safety.

'East Of The Sun'
A song on strummed acoustic guitar with harmonica, describing an early love affair. The melody is hypnotic. It's a mesmerising tender song of love among the sand dunes at Lytham St Annes.

'Tom Tiddler's Ground'
A deceivingly strong song, delivered with gentleness. It features just Roy and acoustic guitars, with Toni Visconti on recorder. Written again in DADGAD tuning – which makes the guitar sing – intricate guitar rhythms maintain the interest. It needs nothing else.

Tom Tiddler's Ground (the place of safety) is a child's game, like tag. Amongst the madness of civilization, there must be somewhere safe to live peacefully with the one you love.

'Francesca'
'Francesca' is a perfect gem of a love song, delivered on acoustic guitar with Roy's unique finger-picking. Like so many of the *Flat Baroque And Berserk* songs, it's a masterful melody that requires no further instrumentation. The production is simple and sufficient. It was written for a beautiful girl with whom Roy spent a memorable night.

'Song Of The Ages'
This song features a harp played by the wonderfully talented Skaila Kanga. She is a beautiful lady who had such presence, holding the studio in awe as she listened to the arrangement, effortlessly playing her accompaniment in just one take. Roy picks the harmonic notes in synchronisation with the harp and then strums the rhythm. The effect of the two instruments together is incredible. The song delivers a Nordic, Viking mood; Roy's voice tender and soothing.

'Song Of The Ages' reminds me of 'Jack Of Hearts': also remarkable, similarly underplayed and produced in a low-key manner. The stunning melody is heroic and bold, with lyrics that match its grandiosity, although the harp and guitar underplay the song's power. Led Zeppelin could have done a magical version of this. It had the potential to be like 'Stairway To Heaven'.

It was written for Mocy and Nick and describes the relationship that was perhaps at its end. Roy is sailing away to the future and leaving them on the shore.

The track featured on the Harvest sampler, *Picnic – A Breath of Fresh Air*.

'Hell's Angels'

EMI were still asking for a single to promote the album. This was strange because there were certainly already a few possibilities. 'Another Day' was the obvious choice, or perhaps shortened versions of 'I Hate The White Man' or 'How Does It Feel'. Failing that, 'East Of The Sun' or even 'Don't You Grieve', would've worked. Why didn't they use one of those?

Roy was resistant to the idea of creating singles. Previous such experiences had not worked out well for him. He disliked producing commercial songs. But in the end and under pressure, he mischievously wrote and recorded 'Hell's Angels': a track that he knew would never be released because it was unsuitable for the media.

'Hell's Angels' was recorded very late at night. The Nice had been performing locally and popped into the studio after their gig. On this track, Roy is having a ball on electric guitar, backed by The Nice for a crazy six-and-a-half-minute romp that was completely improvised after Roy's brief demonstration. They had just completed a practice run when Keith Emerson's girlfriend phoned with an emergency, so he shot off, leaving the track unrecorded. Pete and Roy listened to the practice run and decided to keep it as is. They even left in the blanked-out section at the point that the band lost the rhythm and stopped, leaving just Roy and his electric guitar. He can then be heard leading Blinky, the drummer, back into the rhythm.

The message: Let's have some anarchy!

Needless to say, EMI rejected it, and no single was released.

Outtake
'(It's Tomorrow) And Today Is Yesterday'

This track was considered as a possible single before being dropped. It was similar to superior tracks on the album and required too much work. Featuring Roy on acoustic guitar and harmonica, it would've fitted in quite well, although one lyric section does sound rather clumsy.

It was added – quite incongruously – as a bonus track on the *Come Out Fighting Ghengis Smith* 1991 re-release, and then later on the 2002 album, Today Is Yesterday, that took its name from the song.

Stormcock (1971)

First released on the Harvest label in 1971
Personnel:
Roy Harper: acoustic six and twelve-string guitars and piano and writer of all songs
Pete Jenner: producer
Jimmy Page: acoustic guitar (described as S. Flavius Mercurios) on 'Same Old Rock'
David Bedford: hammond organ and orchestral arrangements.
James Edgar: artwork
Recorded at Abbey Road Studio

Roy continued to enjoy EMI's full backing, although his first album for them had not sold as well as hoped, and no single was forthcoming. He still had Pete Jenner as producer, unlimited studio time, and carte blanche to do what he wanted. Roy revelled in it.

He brought only four tracks to the table for the second album, but what amazing tracks they are. Each of them is an epic, and none is less than seven minutes long. Without a thought for commercial success or singles, Roy and Pete set about creating a monumental album. Each of those four tracks was honed to perfection; each one a work of art. Each, on their own, is worth the price of the album. Together, they produced what is still considered to be Roy's pinnacle of success.

The Smiths' Johnny Marr said of the album: 'If ever there was a secret weapon of a record, it would be *Stormcock* ... It's intense and beautiful and clever: Bowie's Hunky Dory's bigger, badder brother ... *Stormcock* quickly became, and has remained, my favourite album'.

Singer/songwriter Joanna Newsom has said: '*Stormcock* might be my favourite album of all time, an incredible four-song record of epic songs that are filled with incredible innovations, arrangements and recording techniques. A perfect sparkling jewel of a record'.

Despite the album's brilliance, I can imagine the EMI executives on first hearing, asking where the radio play was going to come from or where a single was. Perhaps it was a work of genius, but how was it going to reach the public? Track one's lyrical content exacerbated that problem. 'Hors D'Oeuvres' was unlikely to make many friends in the music press, and without good reviews, the album could not reach a wider audience. Instead of throwing their weight behind the project, the bemused executives allowed it to fizzle out – another lost opportunity.

Stormcock could have and should have been heralded as progressive rock's finest achievement and should've propelled Roy to superstardom. Instead, it languished, largely unnoticed by the wider world.

'Hors D'Oeuvres'
The opening track demonstrates the shift forward in production techniques that Roy and Pete had achieved. Where *Flat Baroque and Berserk* was

beautifully produced but deliberately kept simple, *Stormcock* moves forward into an orchestrated delight of sophistication and style.

'Hors D'Oeuvres' is based on a repeating acoustic guitar refrain, starting very simply with one guitar in standard tuning, then augmented by more guitars, creating a mesmerising, complex assembly of rhythms. Over the top, the voice sings a pattern of six repeating poetic lines. The song gradually builds in speed, intensity and complexity. At the chorus, Roy's voice rises, harmonising in a multitracked choir, creating a symphony of sound.

By verse two, the music has built into an intricate rhythmic wall, with organ supplementing the guitars and a flowing vocal rising above. But the basic structural simplicity is gradually lost in the instrumental intricacy, as the music becomes immensely complex. Chorus two follows a similar pattern to the first, continuing with added Hammond organ flourishes, effects and harmonies.

All told, it is a stunning piece of classical proportions. The eight and a half minutes are like nothing recorded before: a masterpiece of progressive rock music.

The lyrics of the two verses are different. The first – inspired by the story of Caryl Chessman – describes a courtroom scene where the accused is sentenced to death. Chessman was controversially accused of robbery and kidnapping with bodily harm and rape. He was sentenced to death, serving eleven years and ten months on death row, before being executed in 1960. The song highlights the hypocrisy and injustice of the judicial process.

The chorus emphasises, 'You can lead a horse to water, but you're never gonna make him drink/And you can lead a man to slaughter, but you're never gonna make him think'.

Verse two – altogether different – focuses on music critic inadequacies. Roy was stung by a particularly sloppy review that claimed he carped on about all the world's injustices and wrongs without offering a panacea. This verse was his barbed riposte. At gigs, he would actually stop the song part-way through, point at the critics who were often drinking at the bar and not listening, and lambast them royally. These disdainful broadsides did not endear him to the press. But Roy was not concerned in the slightest that his album sales and popularity might depend on those critics and what they wrote about him.

So the album begins with a unique gem, so absorbing and textured that you become lost in it. As the name suggests, 'Hors D'Oeuvres' is just the beginning, and what follows is even more amazing.

'The Same Old Rock'
Track two starts quietly with organ and settles into some duelling guitar. This is Roy playing with Jimmy Page (Jimmy playing under the pseudonym, S. Flavius Mercurios, for contractual reasons).

Roy's voice soars above as the incredible guitars continue their intricate interplay. Roy is playing a twelve-string in standard tuning.

The poem is full of metaphor, with meanings so intricate that to disentangle the lyric and understand its nuances would require much study.

Starting from the perspective of mankind through history, then focussing down to the individual, the poem is partly a reflection on human endeavour and part critique on religion – 'One new sling, the same old rock'. Roy talks about 'The famous straggler stood on the edge of time', who is a religious leader, misleading his gullible followers. The song is written about a time when politics and religion were overtly inseparable.

There is so much in here to think about. Like all good poems, the layers gradually peel away to reveal morality, philosophy and commentary on human existence. The way the poem is married to the music makes the piece comparable to not only the best progressive rock but also classical music. This is truly a work of art.

The short section – when the music drops out, leaving only Roy's voice, pure and expressive – is interesting. Then follows a sublime vocal harmony section, with Roy's many voices weaving through each other, augmented by percussion. The guitars then return with force, settling into a heavy rhythm with immaculate interplay extending to the end's tinkling keyboard, leaving us breathless. This is a song to play and play, to revel in the quality of the music, to ponder over and discover the words' many meanings.

'One Man Rock And Roll Band'

In the zoo that once stood on the Harrods' top floor, Roy introduced himself to one of his more serious girlfriends by saying that he was a one-man rock and roll band. It seems highly appropriate, given the immense sounds just he and his guitar could generate.

The track starts with a unique electrified acoustic guitar, tuned to DADGAD, which is why it feels rather Indian in style. The vocal calls above the strident guitars. With the heavy guitar, Roy really does create a one-man rock and roll band.

This is an anti-war song. The 1960s was during the time of the Vietnam War, a most unpopular war, with soldiers returning home to an antagonistic reception. There are also references to World War I. This was supposed to be the war to end all wars, yet many wars later, the clamour continues.

The lyric also refers to the huge peace rally outside the American embassy in Grosvenor Square, when the usual thugs turned up to turn a peaceful protest into a violent riot. Roy is suggesting how much more effective it might have been if the marchers had walked behind medal-wearing First World War veterans in a united and peaceful demonstration against an unjust war.

The song culminates in a crash of piano – reminiscent of The Beatles' 'A Day In The Life' – before fading out on a drone along with noodling guitar.

Roy mixed this song 'blind' by covering up the board and just following what sounded right! The music, poetry and production, was a stunning achievement.

'Me And My Woman'

The piano crash at the end of 'One Man Rock And Roll Band', still resounds as 'Me And My Woman' begins. This, the album's final track, is another thirteen-minute epic that surely rates as one of Roy's best songs.

It appears to me that this track laid down the template for Pink Floyd's *Dark Side Of The Moon*. Roger Waters would never acknowledge this, but this song – musically and lyrically – was the final piece of the jigsaw for the post-Syd-Barrett Floyd. Roy has never received the credit he deserves.

It begins with multi-layered acoustic guitars, resonating with a rich timbre. Roy's voice is mellow as the melody sets about embellishing the extraordinary poem. As melodies unfurl and the vocal soars through different rhythmic and harmonic sections, the song builds with strings and brass. Roy's vocal harmonies are transcendent: a signature sound for many of his songs, including – with the aid of technology – those in his live solo performances. The changes in tone and rhythm are beautifully orchestrated against the clarinet, piano and strings, giving power and enhancing emotion. The orchestral flow sweeps the mood along. Then guitars come back to the fore, punchier this time, driving forward with repeating riffs. The vocal is now more aggressive but soulfully multitracked on the chorus. The bass underpins the changing pendulum rhythm as the song builds – through multitracked harmonies and orchestration – to a climax before it subsides.

Somehow, thirteen minutes have passed. Never once does the attention waver or the music lose its grip. It flows, soars, and transports us on an absorbing journey – a truly awesome ride of sophisticated complexity and emotion.

And what of the poem that initiated this opus? That also plays with emotion and intellect as it paints thoughts, ideas and stories. On one level, there is the concept of one man facing mankind's fury, its history and warlike culture, but sustained through the refuge of a relationship with a woman. But that scenario – although embroidered with poetic imagery – belies the poem's complexity. The underlying premise is the purity of nature juxtaposed against society's ugly, synthetic structure. Society – epitomised by man's greed and lust for power, control and expansion – produces religion, politics and war. The result is an artificial life played out in this modern world.

Roy and his woman are fighting for their ideals and morality within a culture that is heading for a horrendous doomsday of either complete control or annihilation. It's all there in the lyric – along with a healing touch of love.

Just four songs, but they took progressive rock to new heights of poetic majesty and production. They certainly deserve to be more widely acclaimed.

Lifemask (1973)

First released on the Harvest label in 1973
Personnel:
Pete Jenner: producer
John Leckie: sound technician
Roy Harper: vocals, guitars, synthesiser and bass plus all songwriting
Jimmy Page: lead guitar
Brian Davison: drums on 'The Lord's Prayer'
Tony Carr: bongos
Steve Broughton: bongos
Ray Warley: flute on 'The Lord's Prayer'
Brian Hodges: electric bass on 'Bank of the Dead' and 'The Lord's Prayer'
Laurie Allan: drums on 'Highway Blues'
Recorded at Abbey Road Studio

For Roy, this was a time of frustration, satisfaction, illness, triumph and confusion. He had just produced the magnificent, *Stormcock,* a supreme achievement on so many levels, and he knew it. However, the album didn't sell brilliantly. EMI had not provided enough publicity, and the album was ill-received by both the music press and the general public.

Yet the rock intelligentsia recognized Roy as a major artist. Led Zeppelin, The Who, Jethro Tull, Pink Floyd and Paul McCartney were all dropping into recording sessions, showering Roy with plaudits and singing his praises.

EMI were still in support in a half-hearted way. They still provided studio time, a budget, and Pete Jenner. Now Roy needed to create an album to equal *Stormcock's* brilliance.

Out of left-field came a film opportunity. Roy auditioned for a lead role in the John Mackenzie film, *Made*, co-starring Carol White. Against strong competition from Paul Jones (of Manfred Mann), Roy was given the part. He was to play Mike Preston: a touring rock musician who forms a transient relationship with Carol White's character, Valerie Marshall. Carol was well known at that time, having starred in two successful Ken-Loach-directed social realism films: *Cathy Come Home* and *Poor Cow*. *Made* was going to be a similar type of film. Initially, the idea of becoming a film star energised Roy. But the process soon became tedious and constricting.

EMI were probably wringing their hands with glee. They could see that the prospect of Roy in a major film could lead to a soundtrack and possibly a hit single. Unfortunately, that was not quite the way Roy saw it. Although he reluctantly worked on writing and adapting a few songs for the film, his mind was fixed on a far more adventurous and artistically creative song and album. 'The Lord's Prayer' – along with the other *Lifemask* songs – was already forming in his head.

An even greater problem arose around this time: Roy became ill. Becoming dehydrated, he thought it was the effects of some particularly strong grass he'd been smoking. But it soon became apparent that this was not the cause. He was diagnosed with polycythemia: a glut of red blood cells caused by a blood vessel disorder called haemorrhagic telangiectasia. It was a dangerous condition – blood being shunted through interconnecting blood vessels instead of the lungs. It left Roy short of oxygen, constantly unwell and lacking in energy. Pints of blood had to be removed in order to reduce the red blood corpuscles. He eventually underwent a fairly major operation to close the shunt vessels and redirect the blood flow.

The EMI publicity department needed to keep Roy in the limelight and dreamt up a cock-and-bull story about Roy being ill from giving the kiss of life to a sheep on his farm!

In the heads of EMI and the film executives, Made gave Roy the opportunity to write a film soundtrack: punchy two-and-a-half-minute film songs would be given airplay, propelling both film and album to popular acclaim. But in Roy's head, the film score was a burden. The idea of producing pop songs for the film was anathema. Indeed, he hated the one song he produce for the film: 'Social Casualty', which, with different lyrics, later became 'Bank Of The Dead'. In the film 'Social Casualty' had lyrics about the character Valerie and her baby, but was not included on the album and has never been released.

In the midst of dealing with his illness and making the film, Roy worked on *Lifemask* at Abbey Road, with the help of a supporting cast including Jimmy Page. Roy focussed on the twenty-three-minute epic that would comprise the whole of side two. His medical condition was giving him premonitions of early death. His specialist told him he was not destined to make old bones, and so Roy was determined to pack everything into one great piece of work.

The gatefold cover (designed by James Edgar), which opens centrally, has a 'death mask' of Roy, which is really a life mask. This was symbolic of his cheating death and surviving to make the record – an affirmation of life! Inside the cover was Edgar's red-and-yellow-coloured picture of Geronimo, which sparked the idea for the central part of the poem that became 'The Lord's Prayer'.

Lifemask must have driven the EMI and film executives apoplectic. In no way did it resemble a film soundtrack, and none of the songs – not even 'Bank Of The Dead' – were radio-friendly. They were either too long, too political or contained dubious lyrics, such as the 'shitty city' chorus. What they made of 'The Lord's Prayer' is not known, but I can imagine.

For some inexplicable reason, *Lifemask* was re-released in 1987 on tape, with four incongruous bonus tracks: the two *Folkjokeopus* outtakes – 'Zaney Janey' and 'Ballad Of Songwriter' – the early single, 'Midspring Dithering', and its B-side 'Zengem'. Why anyone thought these in any way fit with the album is beyond me.

'Highway Blues'

'Highway Blues' is a storming song, starting the album with a drone leading into Roy's heavy acoustic guitars, with that DADGAD tuning and its Indian psychedelic feel again. Jimmy Page then comes in with a searing lead. The repeating riff drives the song along, all of the above interspersed with it. The vocal is strong and forceful, on what is probably the best hitch-hiking song ever written, and one that has been a favourite in Roy's live act ever since.

This is him at the side of the road with his thumb out, living free, 'Poaching tomorrow from God and the state', and looking to score a lift from 'the shaven insane'. His girlfriend Margaret (Pia) acts as 'bait'. She is so attractive, 'she pulls like a train'!

We are back to Roy's wild days of hitching through Europe, living outside of society, with different values to most people; a lifestyle that created strange situations through living a parallel life while scrounging off the society that was being rejected.

The track builds in intensity as it moves towards the last verse, the orchestral accompaniment adding to the crescendo.

Wow!! A rocking start to the album and a totally different vibe to that of *Stormcock*; six and a half minutes of power.

'All Ireland'

Next is a soft, melodic ode to Ireland, with harmonica in the background, and Roy on acoustic guitar, delivering a delicate emotional vocal.

Cradled in a haunting melody, 'All Ireland' is a political song that urges the Irish to rise above their nationalist slogans and religious lies, to create a less-divided society. It's certainly a contrast to 'Highway Blues', in both style and content.

'Little Lady'

'Little Lady': a tragic and painful episode from Roy's early life, full of emotion and bitterness, is a personal homage to his first love. Its lyric has a different perspective to 'East Of The Sun' but is about Roy and the same girlfriend, their intense young love, and the tragedy that followed. Her parents did not approve of the relationship, and when the song's little lady became pregnant, they forced her to terminate and the young lovers to part.

A bed of acoustic guitars gradually builds in passion as it projects mounting emotion beneath the lilting vocal. The song ends on a long fading note.

'Bank Of The Dead'

When first recorded for the film, *Made*, this song had different lyrics and was titled 'Social Casualty'. That was rewritten as 'Bank Of The Dead', with the intention of giving EMI the single they wanted. The track has the full works, with strong production, effects, and a band featuring Jimmy Page on guitar.

Although the lyric is concerned with Roy's favourite subjects – the suffocating society (with swipes at religion and wealth seekers) and the growing control of people – he hated it. Not even Jimmy's guitar solos could redeem it for Roy. He went as far as putting a strong magnet in the master tape box so that gradually over the course of time, the recording would be ruined. Perhaps he found the song's possible single release to be a problem. Or was it the association with 'Social Casualty'? Either way, the chorus of 'Shitty city shitty city' was sufficient to annoy EMI executives and ensure zero radio airplay.

'South Africa'
Another political masterpiece with the guitar tuned to DADGAD: a complete contrast to the previous track. Roy harmonises with himself over delicate acoustic picking.

South Africa was in the depths of apartheid, and change was needed. Roy would sometimes dedicate this song to his black 'brothers', declaring that minds are not changed with anger. He would recite the lyric, whispering 'South Africa' and 'English' in the appropriate places, ending with, 'One day she might come to understand that apartheid is total bullshit'. The ending wends its way through a delightful filigree of notes.

'The Lord's Prayer'
Side one is an eclectic mix of excellent tracks. But the tour de force is the 23-minute track taking up the entire side two. There is always debate and disagreement, but 'The Lord's Prayer' ranks up there with 'McGoohan's Blues', 'Me And My Woman', 'The Game' and 'I Hate The White Man'.

At the time, his prospects did not look good, and he was suffering from a serious condition that might put an end to his singing and possibly his life. The consultant had not minced his words, leaving Roy with no doubt as to the seriousness of the situation. It was a time of immense ups and downs, just like the poem itself. There had been the artistic achievement of *Stormcock*, but its lack of commercial success; beckoning fame via a major film role, but Roy's rejection of show business; and the soaring of his artistic abilities, but his failing health. A strange period in his life indeed; but out of this, another masterpiece emerged.

Roy poured everything into 'The Lord's Prayer', wanting it to encapsulate all he felt and stood for. It started as a poem called 'Lifeboat', which is the first part of the song. But then he became stuck. With the help of LSD, a 14-hour writing session and James Edgar's Geronimo picture, the central poem was created. He then grafted another song onto the end, creating the final piece – his magnum opus.

In many ways, 'The Lord's Prayer' was a straight evolution from *Come Out Fighting Ghengis Smith*. Making the opening poem delivery riveting enough to encourage repeated listenings took skill from both Roy and producer Pete Jenner. Jimmy Page's immaculately-timed guitar (recorded in one single take) truly transformed the central poem's repeating refrain into something special. The fabulous production, harmonies, and vocals augmenting the poem brought the whole to life as a musical wonder.

This epic is broken down into five distinct sections.

'Poem'
'Modal Song Parts I-IV'
'Front Song'
'Middle Song'
'End Song (Front Song Reprise)'

The poem is difficult to dissect, as its range is immense: full of metaphors, polarities and variations in rhythm, and covering the scope of human history, touching on superstition and the inevitability of our demise.

The opening section (initially called 'Lifeboat') sets the scene. The words are something to become lost in; to ponder and decipher with pleasure, as various meanings are uncovered. Like a jigsaw, they come together to create a picture. Music flowing in at the poetry section's end sends shivers down the spine as the second poem – 'Geronimo' – begins.

Roy is talking of mankind's potential as glimpsed in the life of Geronimo: the glory of human lives when freed from repression. Resenting control in any form, Roy saw society as claustrophobic. He would have preferred to live life as a free man on the American plains: hunting, riding and experiencing the full gamut of life – the highs and the lows. When James Edgar handed over that coloured Geronimo photo, Roy found himself peering into the eyes and mind of a man who had lived the stone-age life that Roy himself craved. Under the influence of acid, he thought he understood everything that motivated Geronimo.

The guitar plays an incredible repeating coda, over which the poem is recited/sung, with background harmonies adding bite. The vocal's rise and fall maintain interest while the guitar creates a simply mesmerising circular flow.

We are in the mind of a stone-age warrior – his strength, philosophy and motivation, revealed. Each line provokes thought and understanding. The rhythm picks up in speed as the backing increases in complexity, taking us up with it. Attention is maintained through the developing instrumentation and rhythmic changes.

The poor planet is the 'big lady' we're playing with.

As the piece slows, the harmonies build and build, and slowly we bridge through to the final section. No longer in Geronimo's mind, we are in a classroom, as children, mindful of the world and its possibilities. Roy is looking out the window and longing for freedom.

We are now in an altogether different song. As the massed destructive armies of flawed mankind, rampage across the planet, is it too late to create a world with care?

There is the faintest hint of optimism. I cannot think of any other piece of music/poem that takes one on such a journey: an incredible achievement and another stunning album.

Single
'Bank Of The Dead' b/w 'Little Lady'
Two tracks from the album.

Alternative Tracks in the Film *Made*
'Social Casualty (Valerie's Song)'
A less produced, largely acoustic version of 'Bank Of The Dead'. A live version with different lyrics – titled 'Valerie's Song' – is used in the film, where the track was played over the radio as Valerie (Carol White) listens and cries. The alternative lyric is about Valerie's life, her dead child, and the circumstances she finds herself in.

Valentine (1974)

First released on the Harvest label in 1974
Personnel:
Pete Jenner: producer
Roy Harper: guitar, vocals and all song writing (apart from North Country)
Jimmy Page: electric guitar on 'Male Chauvinist Pig Blues'
Keith Moon: drums on 'Male Chauvinist Pig Blues'
Ronnie Lane: bass on 'Male Chauvinist Pig Blues'
Mike Gibbs: brass arrangement on 'Male Chauvinist Pig Blues'
Ian Anderson: flute on 'Home'
David Bedford: orchestral arrangement
Steve Broughton: percussion
Pete Sears: bass on 'Forbidden Fruit' and 'Acapulco Gold'
Max Middleton: piano on 'Acapulco Gold'
Marty Simon: drums on 'Acapulco Gold'
Tim Walker: guitar on 'Che'
John Leckie: sound engineer
Recorded at Abbey Road Studio
Cover art: Joe Petagno
Highest UK chart place: 27

The idea for *Valentine* was to release an album of love songs on Valentine's Day. He had written many haunting love songs in his time, and an album of these beautiful melodies would surely please EMI.

A great launch gig to celebrate the album's release was planned to occur at Finsbury Park's Rainbow Theatre. It was called the Valentine's Day Massacre and featured The Intergalactic Elephant Band: Roy on vocal and electric guitar, Jimmy Page on lead guitar, Ronnie Lane on bass, Keith Moon on drums, John Bonham bouncing around with acoustic guitar, with Robert Plant supporting them from the wings.

The *Valentine* album is actually not made up of pure love songs. Roy did not stick to the script, extending the love song genre to include all manner of topics: young love, sex, male chauvinism, communal living, enjoyment of dope, a tribute to a hero, appreciation of the natural world, and women's liberation, as well as including the passions churning around in relationship break-ups. However, the result was a great album with a number of exceptional songs.

In 1989, *Valentine* was re-released, on Awareness Records, with three bonus tracks – lifted from Flashes From The Archives Of Oblivion – featuring The Intergalactic Elephant Band: 'Home' (studio version), 'Home' (live) and 'Too Many Movies'.

'Forbidden Fruit'

This song, about an intense love affair in Roy's youth, captures both the ardour of young love and the overpowering passion of burgeoning sexuality.

The tune is delightful with exquisite picked guitar and a melody reminiscent of 'Forever', with Roy's voice at its most gentle. As the song progresses, a fuller sound emerges, with first more guitars and bass, leading to an orchestral flourish, ending with a chorus of young girls' voices.

'Male Chauvinist Pig Blues'

Part satire and partly based in truth, this song provides a wilful view of what constitutes a love song. Here, Roy is in angry mode, in the throes of a relationship break-up, portraying himself as a male chauvinist pig and throwing his weight around. He describes his home background as a pitched battle with his religious stepmother. He is in search of love and a relationship but admits he is selfish enough to only want this on his terms. If he found the right lady, maybe then everything would be different.

The track is a stormer, based on a fabulous riff: one that really comes to the fore in live performance when played with two duelling acoustic guitars. This album version features the most amazing electric supergroup: Keith Moon on drums, Jimmy Page on electric guitar and Ronnie Lane on bass – though there is some debate about the latter. Ronnie certainly was in the live band and is credited in some sources as also being on the album. Others claim Roy played the bass himself. Not that it matters much – the track rocks. Just listen to that bass laying it down, then the duelling guitars playing an amazing riff against Moon's superb drums. Roy is in top form, vocally – so powerful.

'I'll See You Again'

At last, we reach (what appears at first to be) a genuine love song. Certainly, there is tenderness and beauty in its delivery, but that conflicts with the lyric's harsher reality.

When singer, Bonnie Prince Billy, played it for his girlfriend, she immediately hated the lyric – she saw that it disguised a brutal message. He said: 'It never occurred to me.'

It is the story of the relationship break-up of the *Made* film couple, played by Roy and his co-star, Carol White. It harshly portrays Carol's character as a needy person wanting a permanent relationship. Roy – reluctant to be tied down – rebels against this. Monogamous relationships, kids and humdrum living were anathema to him.

Superb acoustic guitar accompanies soulful vocals. Then a restrained bass and lavish strings send the song soaring. The song is beautifully conceived and constructed but is another massively underrated track. The end result was a work of art, whatever the sentiments.

'Twelve Hours Of Sunset'

A love song to the planet? To nature? To the wonder of life? I'm not quite sure how this one fits the love theme. But it's one of Roy's best songs – a dreamy poem describing a flight from London to Los Angeles. A flight that follows the setting sun for twelve hours creates a weird illusion in which time stops and – like a neutrino – arrival occurs before departure. Madness and unreality conspire to create this picture of wonder as the planet puts on its light show.

A sympathetic orchestra and soft harmonies augment Roy and his guitars, his voice soaring majestically above. The ending's intertwining harmonies are sublime. Another gem.

'Acapulco Gold'

In the context of the album, I suppose this is a love song to hash. Roy has never hidden his love of marijuana, which has often made him a target for critics.

'Acapulco Gold' is a zany favourite from his stage act, where he would loon it up for laughs. This time, Max Middleton (piano), Marty Simon (drums) and Pete Sears (bass) deliver it in a mellow jazz, with just the right lounge lizard feel, as Roy slips into stoned reverie.

'Commune'

At last, a genuine love song with no barbs or hidden meaning. It's an utterly delightful outpouring of love. Roy picks his way through, the guitar in standard tuning, as David Bedford's orchestral arrangement tastefully augments and builds tension.

Roy is reflecting on those ideal summer days of love – with Pia in Norway and Nancy in England – surrounded by nature. He combines those memories with a wish to see all his friends and lovers gathered together under one roof. Somewhere out there, the perfect love waits. It's an ode to the wonder of love, past, present and future.

'Magic Woman (Liberation Reshuffle)'

This crazy song is yet another interpretation of love, in a rollicking negative spin on the Women's liberation movement. It is implied that female power is responsible for civilisation, including the benefits and downsides.

It's one of Roy's zany experimental efforts that doesn't quite work for me. Yet it is an interesting piece because of its dynamic excursion into weirdness, with some of Roy's excellent acoustic electricity. Nobody plays guitar like him. The percussion and bass complete the full band sound. The end is a mad party with all the atmosphere of a carnival, a full chorus, and the assertion that 'We're gonna change the whole world around'. Something 'we' only part-managed.

'Che'

Another love interpretation and an instrumental where Roy demonstrates his acoustic guitar prowess in a variety of ways. It's a 'descendant' of 'Blackpool' and 'One For All' and a song of admiration for South American revolutionary Che Guevara.

'North Country' (Traditional – Arr. Roy Harper)

Bob Dylan stole Martin Carthy's arrangement of this old English folk song, renamed it 'Girl From The North Country', and claimed it as his own. Roy was here stealing it back. At the time, I think they expected that the Dylan camp might react, but they didn't. Simon and Garfunkel adapted their take on 'Scarborough Fair' from the same Martin Carthy version.

This was the first time Roy recorded anything he hadn't written. But with his northern roots, this song had a particular resonance with him.

He sings with great tenderness and simplicity, the orchestra enhances his guitar without ever overpowering. In concert, Roy would often mimic Dylan's drawl for the first verse.

'Forever'

This is a lavish and rich re-recording of the song from *Sophisticated Beggar*. The vocal is warm and tender, the instrumental backing full and polished. It was written for Mocy, and is one of his loveliest songs. I enjoy this, although I prefer the raw original version. But it was certainly a good choice to end this album with.

Single
'(Don't You Think We're) Forever' b/w 'Male Chauvinist Pig Blues (Live)'

'Forever' is taken from the album but 'Male Chauvinist Pig Blues' is an acoustic live version, with Jimmy Page playing some exquisite slide guitar.

HQ (1975)

First released on the Harvest Label in 1975
Personnel:
Pete Jenner: producer
Roy Harper: vocals, acoustic guitar and all songwriting
Chris Spedding: lead guitar
Dave Cochran: bass guitar
Bill Bruford: drums, percussion
Dave Gilmour: lead guitar on 'The Game'
John Paul Jones: bass guitar on 'The Game'
Steve Broughton: drums and percussion on 'The Game'
The Grimethorpe Colliery band on 'When An Old Cricketer Leaves The Crease'.
Artwork: Hipgnosis
Photography: Po Powell
Recorded at Abbey Road Studio
Highest UK chart place: 31

Once again, an album cover caused controversy. Roy's American label, Chrysalis, deemed the Hipgnosis image of him walking on water, unsuitable for US release. In the end, the album was released under the title of one of its songs – 'When An Old Cricketer Leaves The Crease' – the front cover featuring a photo of Roy topless in cricket gear, with the rules of cricket on the back.

A promotional ad – showing Roy with a big head, standing in front of a bull with a pile of bull shit – also caused a stir. This also backfired.

If the myth of Roy being a folk singer was ever to be dispelled, this was the moment. He used his Hyde Park band in the studio to record opening track, 'The Game': they were hard-hitting, out-and-out rock. Of that, there is no doubt.

Roy collected chords, styles and genres, like a magpie: jazz, folk, rock, eastern, avant-garde, classical, Gregorian chant, brass band, music hall – an eclectic mix. Blending them with his own inventions, he created something unique. On this album, rock is very much to the fore, but his wide range of inspiration is evident. Everything is there.

To complete the record, Roy put together a band he named Trigger: the name of Roy Rogers' horse. Perhaps the name signified Roy Harper's maverick character? Strange – I'd associate Roy more with Indians than cowboys.

Trigger were a cracking rock band with a heavy brand of rock and roll, yet capable of subtlety, as on 'Hallucinating Light' or 'When An Old Cricketer Leaves The Crease'. They were consummate professionals. Guitarist Chris Spedding especially – with his rock and roll background and hard rock sensitivities – gave the band a hard edge.

In addition to Spedding (formerly of Sharks, fresh from playing with The Wombles, and soon to be involved with the Sex Pistols), there was session bassist Dave Cochran and drummer Bill Bruford (King Crimson and Yes): an experienced group.

After recording the album, Roy and Trigger took to the road for a series of gigs, where they demonstrated that they could really rock the joint. But touring was a costly business, and they ran at a loss. After over-exerting himself in many different directions (some of them chemical), Roy collapsed on stage. Out of action for quite a while, this put an end to Trigger.

During the making of *HQ*, Pink Floyd were recording what was to become *Wish You Were Here* in the studio next door, and Roy was invited to record the vocal on 'Have A Cigar'. He even toured and performed live with Pink Floyd on a few occasions.

Roy was now riding high: at the very peak of his career and songwriting, heralded by many major rock acts (The Who, Pink Floyd, Led Zeppelin, Jethro Tull). It only seemed a matter of time before he would experience similar stardom. He just needed the right record, a good single and a push from EMI. Perhaps this was it?

'The Game (Parts 1-5)'

Right from the opening guitar chords, we are in for a powerful album. There's no easing into it and no gentle or humorous tracks preceding or following epics as he had often done before. Dave Gilmour, John Paul Jones and Bill Bruford really pack some heavy artillery. That riff is a monster that thuds through you like The Kinks' 'You Really Got Me', setting your heart thumping.

At just under fourteen minutes long (short by Roy's standards), this epic has immense impact. Here he married acoustic music's soft nuances to rock's brash hardness, creating a masterpiece of variation and mood. The first four minutes consist of that heavy repeating riff. Then the pace changes to gentle, lyrical section before speeding up a little. There is a variety of instrumentation, including xylophone. By around nine minutes in, the heavy guitar returns, building on the earlier riff, augmented by harmonies and echo. A protracted instrumental section then rollicks along at pace beneath Chris Spedding's scintillating slide guitar. The heavy returning riff signals the end, as Roy sings, 'Please leave this world as clean as when you came': he was at pains to explain that this was not a plea on behalf of the Keep Britain Tidy campaign.

The poem restates Roy's basic premise that civilisation is not a good idea. Somehow, way back in the distant past, we gave up our natural way of life as hunter-gatherers and allowed ourselves to be controlled. We are now cocooned in a claustrophobic society run by a powerful elite. It's a game of greed and power. We can't change it. All we can do is dream of a place to call our own, where we can find love. But – with an echo of The Prisoner – there really is nowhere outside of the game, and we're all in it together whether we like it or not. We're all sponsors of this hell. We can only do our best to not make it worse.

'The Spirit Lives'

Track two continues in the same vein, Trigger creating a vibe similar to the Gilmour/Jones/Broughton band that had played in the park. It's another powerful song – a broadside at religion. The poem's basis is that civilisation created powerful gods to sanctify an authoritative elite and keep populations subservient. It was a powerful tool, not only of control but for inciting expansion, war and conquest: a mechanism to spread intolerance and hate.

With lines like 'Goodness lives where God is dead', the lyric was likely to generate strong reactions. But then, Roy has never shied away from controversy nor sought an easy path. Popularity was never his motivating force. He says it how he feels it, and he feels that religion – and Christianity in particular – plays a huge part in not only controlling but subjugating people and was part of the nail hammered into the coffin of freedom, destroying old tribal ways and implementing hierarchy and control. The old religions – the worship of nature and the Green Man – were cruelly suppressed and eradicated.

The song ends on the positive decree that love is the antidote to religion; the spirit lives; the shackles of religion will be shucked off.

'Grown Ups Are Just Silly Children'

Side one ends in rock and roll madness. Chris Spedding gives the song the complete rock treatment. Though a bit of a throwaway, it's great fun and should have been a hit. But even in his most frivolous songs, Roy usually includes a barbed message. Sex, drugs and rock 'n' roll – we're sleepwalking into a disaster. It's time we grew up.

'Referendum (Legend)'

Side two begins with another slab of solid rock. Chris Spedding's guitar is biting, searing and cutting, delivering another great riff to drive you crazy and get your head banging. Bruford and Cochran provide a solid backing, Roy sounding confident and relaxed in the rock setting: in fact, he's loving it. The energy of Led Zeppelin and The Who has rubbed off on him. He sees himself as a rock star. But then, he always has been. This was apparent right from the first album – *Sophisticated Beggar* – which had a full band rock treatment on the song, 'Committed'.

'Referendum' is a hard rock rework of the first album's 'Legend', but with different lyrics. At the time, the UK was involved in a referendum over joining the European Union, or 'common market' as it was then known. The man from 'Muddlebro' is Ted Heath, who, with arrogant superiority, negotiated the terms of entry and agreed on a poor deal. As the politicians yapped, real life went on. Nothing changes. In our current times of Brexit, this song can be interpreted in a different context.

'Forget Me Not'

Now we get a change of mood. While not being one of Roy's best love songs, it is an interesting and quality track and some of the production techniques used on previous Harper/Jenner productions return. Choral harmonies, acoustic guitars, a delicate underlying bass and extensive multitracking create a symphonic effect.

'Hallucinating Light'

Here we are treated to another of Roy's very best pieces: a fabulous love song with mystical overtones and poetic layering.

This take was actually a rehearsal, but everyone nailed it so perfectly, it was used for the album. Chris Spedding's guitar tone perfectly matches Roy's subdued vocal, building on Bill Bruford and Dave Cochran's faultless base. I'm not sure who the organist is, but it fits seamlessly. Roy is flying! – his vocal expressive; its delivery incredibly atmospheric. After the heavy rock of 'The Game' and 'Referendum' this is a great contrast, but the rock ethic is still there.

Basically, it's a love poem put to music. I love the imagery in a song full of social observation and mysticism. The line, 'Whilst the sick majority still infest the myths of doom', comments on our sad society. But he goes on to suggest that lovers can comfort each other in this darkness, and reach for answers and sometimes find understanding; 'But then it slips away'.

That fabulous end line – 'When I cry... it's you' – never fails to get me: beautifully delivered.

'When An Old Cricketer Leaves The Crease'

It's one brilliant song after another, and this is certainly a masterpiece. Ostensibly a song about cricket, the track is also a metaphor for life and death. It's an evocative piece, summoning up those lazy summer days spent watching the 'chess game' of cricket, slowly and intensely played out on the village green. It could be Geoffrey Boycott facing John Snow, or it could be John Peel and John Walters falling out of 'the game', as we all will. It captures a time that is slowly slipping away and may already be gone.

The guitar has standard tuning, and Roy uses many Major seven chords to obtain that dreamy effect.

This superbly beautiful song starts with sparse, perfectly-timed acoustic guitar. The vocal – intense and full of emotion – gradually builds and rises but never loses the ethereal vibe. Double-tracking subtly adds body before the Grimethorpe Colliery Band (superbly arranged by David Bedford) comes in, taking the music to another level.

The last verse is delivered in plaintiff harmonies. With harmonica in the background, the band mimics the refrain, Roy's voice oozing emotion. Our lives – glimpsed through the vapours of a glass of real ale – are much more than just 'yarns of their day'. One day, we shall all fade away to become ghosts.

I guess our ripples go on. John Peel dedicated it to John Walters after his death, and Nik Kershaw played it for John Peel. I'm hoping that someone will play it at a celebration of my life.

Singles

'When An Old Cricketer Leaves The Crease' b/w 'Hallucinating Light (Acoustic)'

The A-side should have been a massive hit but sadly did not receive the push and exposure it deserved.

'Hallucinating Light' is here an acoustic version. It's not as compelling as the album version, but still a great interpretation: a well-written song can stand all manner of styles and treatments. The song does the work – robust enough to survive any approach: this is what defines Roy's many classics.

'Grown Ups Are Just Silly Children' b/w 'Referendum (Legend)'

Both taken from the album.

Why these singles were not hits, is a mystery.

In 1995, *HQ* was re-released on Roy's Science Friction label, with added bonus tracks: 'The Spirit Lives (Early mix – 23/3/75)', 'When An Old Cricketer Leaves The Crease' (Live in Exeter – 31/10/77)', and ''Hallucinating Light (7' single version)'.

Bullinamingvase (1977)

First released on the Harvest label in 1977
Pete Jenner: producer
Roy Harper: vocals, guitars and all songwriting
'Admiral' John Halsey: drums
Henry McCullough: guitars
Andy Roberts: guitars, backing vocals
Dave Lawson: keyboards
Jimmy McCulloch: guitars
B. J. Cole: pedal steel guitar
Percy Jones: bass guitar
Alvin Lee: guitar on 'One Of Those Days In England'
Ronnie Lane: bass on 'One Of Those Days In England' and 'Watford Gap'
Dave Cochran: bass
Herbie Flowers: bass
Max Middleton: keyboards
Steve Broughton: drums
Skaila Kanga: harp
Linda McCartney: backing vocals on 'One Of Those Days In England'
Paul McCartney: backing vocals on 'One Of Those Days In England'
Dave Plowman: euphonium, trombone
The Vauld Symphony Orchestra: arranged by Roy Harper, conducted by Dave Lawson
John Leckie: sound engineer
Mark Vigars: sound engineer
Recorded at Vauld Farm
Artwork: Hipgnosis
Highest UK chart place: 25

The album was released in the US as *One Of Those Days In England*. Thanks to Led Zeppelin manager, Peter Grant, Roy was at this time living at Vauld Farm: a timber farmhouse (dating back to 1500) near Hereford, with two and a half acres of land, outbuildings and stables. He was half-heartedly trying his hand at farming.

Rather than traipse up to Abbey Road studio, he decided to record the album down on the farm, cadging equipment and staff from EMI, to set up a temporary studio of his own. The musicians dropped in, made their contributions, and no doubt enjoyed a good time.

Following Trigger's demise (Chris Spedding and Bill Bruford going their own ways), Roy formed a new band: Chips. They formed the kernel of musicians featured on the album.

'Admiral' John Halsey: drums (Lou Reed, The Rutles), Andy Roberts: guitar, backing vocals (The Scaffold, Liverpool Scene, Plainsong), Dave Lawson:

keyboards (Greenslade, Stackridge), Henry McCullough: guitar (Spooky Tooth, Grease Band, Wings), Dave Cochran: bass (Trigger).

The band was later renamed Black Sheep. Without Spedding and Bruford, they lost their steely-hard rock sound as Chips/Black Sheep were more sophisticated. But what they lacked in power, they made up for in craft.

With such a large cast, a homemade studio and a relaxed party atmosphere, there was a danger that the finished album might lack cohesion. But this did not end up being the case. Quality and consistency are apparent throughout *Bullinamingvase*. It's is up there with Roy's very best work, vying with *Stormcock*, *Lifemask* and *HQ* for top billing.

As before, the two album sides were distinct. Side one consisted of shorter songs, three of them outstanding. But it is side two that was exceptional. With 'One Of Those Days In England (Parts 2-10)', Roy crafted one of his classic epics: a song that would stand up against 'McGoohan's Blues', 'I Hate The White Man', 'Me and My Woman', 'The Game' and 'The Lord's Prayer'. The song placed *Bullinamingvase* on a par with Roy's best albums.

There was high expectation for the album. It was felt that if the 'One Of Those Days In England' single hit the charts, it could be the breakthrough they'd been looking for. Everyone agreed that both single and album had commercial potential. The band were poised. An agreement had been made with *Top Of The Pops*, that if the single breached the top 30, they were on. Everyone was geared up, and there was tension. But sadly, it all came to nothing.

Some bright spark of an executive had the strange idea of enclosing the single along with the album. This had the immediate effect of dampening the single's sales. Consequently, it stalled at 42 in the charts, and the Top Of The Pops appearance never happened.

'One Of Those Days In England'
This single was produced as an attempt at the charts. Roy transformed the catchy segment of 'One Of Those Days In England (Parts 2-10)' into something that could easily have troubled the top 30. With slide guitar, strings, warm backing vocals, brass section and bright production, it was a promising proposition. With Roy never brilliant at producing commercial product, for once, his antipathy didn't stop him from producing a potentially successful recording. However...

Perhaps the sex and drug references were too inhibiting?
Perhaps it was the physical single being included with the album?
Perhaps it was the general anti-Harper attitude of critics and media?
Perhaps it was for the best?
If Roy had become hugely successful, it might've changed him as a person. We might not have enjoyed all those extraordinary gigs from the 1980s to the present, or indeed all those later gems of albums. Who knows?

'These Last Days'

From the first gentle guitar flourishes, it is clear that Black Sheep had a totally different vibe to Trigger. This is delicate and ethereal, with all the sensibilities of a love song – although it is not just a love song. Roy wistfully acknowledges that perhaps it is pointless to rail against society; that confrontations cannot be won and resistance is futile. He recognises that all sides have their faults. He is hoping to find fulfilment in love and reconcile himself to a peaceful life in a quiet corner. He's looking for contentment and is in love again – this time with Verna Elizabeth, who will feature in a few more songs.

The band enhances Roy's pensive performance through sensitive arrangements evoking summer days, tender love, and escape from the world into a cocoon of peace. The instrumentation is complex, the floating harp giving a dreamy quality, enhanced by the band members' background vocals. Even the busy sections retain the serene quality, the track reaching its climax with the purr of contentment intact.

'Cherishing The Lonesome'

Track three follows, in a similar vein, with a sophisticated backing, softer than that of *HQ*. The guitar is tuned to DADGAD, showing echoes of 'South Africa'.

The first three verses follow a pattern and are almost recited over the placid backing. Then the electric guitar heralds a change of mood – the chorus with a heavier riff, the vocal reaching for the heights.

Roy is introspective, lying in bed listening to the rain and brooding, reaching for the spiritual but still desiring of lust and animalism. He seeks perfection through relationship after relationship but acknowledges that he constantly falls short. Once again, he is contemplating a relationship's end.

Then a gentler mood – like the earlier verses – returns. This time, an electric guitar plays the melody. Roy is wondering if there will ever be someone to share his journey.

'Naked Flame'

'Naked Flame' is an exceedingly strong but rather strange offering. The country feel and understated pedal steel seem at odds with the poem sentiments, but it works. Reminding me of Pink Floyd's 'Wish You Were Here', 'Naked Flame' sounds like a Dave Gilmour song that Roger Waters has slowed down. The riff is similar and in standard tuning.

This lyric is a sad reflection on the painful break-up with Nancy. Following some acrimony, she had walked out, taking their child Stefan with her. Initially, Roy feels grief, sorrow and regret. Reflecting back on the heights of their love, he is contemplating the 'savage god' of suicide, in disbelief of how it could've descended into such bitterness.

The final verse ends in a more upbeat tone (now that time has passed). There are new goals to aim for, new loves to seek: 'But through old destruction flies new dawn/And I rode the winds into the morn'.

'Watford Gap'

This arrangement of Lonnie Donegan's skiffle standard, 'Cumberland Gap', is one of Roy's comical, tongue-in-cheek offerings – complete with banjo and mouth harp. He had great fun putting these lyrics together: football hooligans, Chopper Ronnie Harris, goolies, stagnant wombs, syphilitic whores, yodelling up the canyon (oral sex), concrete burgers and used bathwater. I can't imagine what Watford Gap's Blue Boar Inn found to complain about.

Watford Gap was where bands and football fans used to end up late at night and was one of the few places that stayed open at the time. You could say they did not serve Cordon bleu. Roy would go into the Blue Boar Inn and order strange combinations, such as kippers and custard.

'The Watford Gap, Watford Gap, a plate of grease and a load of crap', went the captivating chorus, and I bet many people still sing it as they pass through Watford Gap to this day.

But The Blue Boar Inn threatened to sue EMI and Roy. One of their owners happened to be on the EMI board and kicked up a fuss. Roy wanted to ask renowned food critic, Egon Ronay, to substantiate his claims about the food quality, but EMI were against him doing so. So after much debate, it was decided to remove the track from future *Bullinamingvase* pressings and replace it with the innocuous 'Breakfast With You'.

'Breakfast With You'

A throwaway track of little significance, based on a laddish chat-up line that Roy and Jimmy Page used: passing girls a note, asking whether they might like to join them for breakfast.

This track differs in style from the rest of the album, bringing the drums to the fore and using the bass to create a jazz feel. Perhaps it was another shot at a single that did not make the grade?

'One Of Those Days In England (Parts 2-10)'

Although side one does have some important numbers (a fun track and a slightly iffy single), side two is once again the main event.

This 19-and-a-half-minute epic is one of Roy's greatest songs. The political humour and opening-section drug and sex references guaranteed the song nil airplay (not that the length would even allow for it). But to Roy's loyal fans, it is one of his most revered songs.

The nine sections are all unique. The instrumentation is sophisticated and varied, ranging from heavy driving riffs to delicate acoustic sections. The guitars' power stems from the DADGAD tuning. The vocal delivery demonstrates the complete range of Roy's expression.

Once again, it's an epic progressive rock track that challenges classical music in its complexity. The content is impressive. The lyric/poem dwells on the full spectrum of human experience, from our history to our future conquest of space. One of the themes is the mad expansion and control exerted on society, often resulting in violence and terrorism. Another is the futility of resistance to such a global system. Roy juxtaposes these themes against the healing power of nature: extending to include the universe and infinity. Our history, lives and times, are slowly fading into the past – taking all we have cherished. Soon we shall all be gone, along with our dearly-held beliefs. The song ends on a positive note: we have time enough to make the most of what we have, to live and love in the moment and enjoy life.

Part of the pleasure of any poem is unpicking its meaning and inspiration, and there's plenty in this one.

'One Of Those Days In England (Parts 2-10)' is a mammoth accomplishment. Roy Harper at the very peak of his powers.

Singles
'One Of Those Days In England (Part 1)' b/w 'Watford Gap'. Released 1977.
Lifted from the album, a pop single aimed at the charts – with a fair bit of Roy's rebellious cheek. It should have been a hit.

'Sail Away' b/w 'Cherishing The Lonesome'. Released 1977.
How quickly Roy moves on. He was already working on the next album even at the release of *Bullinamingvase*, which could've benefitted from some promotion.

'Sail Away' is a track from the next intended album – *Commercial Breaks (Doesn't It?)* – which was still in its early stages (and would ultimately be rejected and left unreleased for many years). As such, I have dealt with it further along under that album. Why the song was selected as a single at this point is a mystery – it's a strange choice.

The B-side – 'Cherishing The Lonesome' – taken from *Bullinamingvase*, is a strong song and should surely have been the A-side. It would have helped promote that album, with 'Sail Away' best held back until its album was ready. But there was pressure from EMI, and it was easier to give them what they wanted. This illustrates how confused EMI were in marketing and managing Roy's career. They could have been so much wiser in their decision-making.

'When An Old Cricketer Leaves The Crease' b/w 'Home'. Released 1978.
Two old singles that had been previously released. The A-side was a superb track that should've been a hit. I can understand it being released again if EMI were looking to give it a big push, but there was no evidence of that. It was merely a stopgap to fill a vacuum.

Conclusion
Bullinamingvase was another masterpiece, allowed to slip by without adequate promotion. I don't think EMI knew how to market Roy at all. They

recognised his talent and potential but were unable to make him a commercial success. It was difficult: his music lacked wide mass-market appeal. There was, however, a niche market of discerning listeners. Perhaps that was all there ever could be? It appears that only a minority of people truly appreciate quality.

Commercial Breaks (Doesn't it?) (1977)

Planned for the Harvest label in 1977 but unreleased
Released on Science Friction label 1994
Personnel:
Roy Harper/Pete Jenner: producer
Roy Harper: vocals, guitar and all songwriting
Dave Cochrane: bass guitar
'Admiral' John Halsey: drums
Dave Lawson: keyboards
Henry McCullough: electric guitar
Andy Roberts: guitars
John Leckie: sound engineer
Recorded: Abbey Road studios, East Grinstead (Jethro Tull Rehearsal Studio),
Rockfield, Vauld Farm, Chapel Lane, The Workhouse.

EMI now put the pressure on. They wanted a follow-up to *Bullinamingvase*,
they wanted singles and they wanted success. But it wasn't quite happening.
But they acknowledged their mistakes, desirous of a further opportunity to
make it work, and once again promised the earth.

Roy produced some demos, but by this time, the music business had changed
considerably. Punk had blown the market awry. EMI were losing money:
their whole vision was off course. There was little interest in the progressive
rock market they had been promoting, and their artists were now labelled
as dinosaurs. All media attention was given to the new boys: Sex Pistols, The
Clash, The Damned and The Stranglers.

Confidence in Roy was evaporating fast. There was a row over the new
album's funding, studio time, promotion and marketing. Recording occurred
in a number of different studios (of varying quality), and Roy finally offered
some semi-completed tracks. EMI were not happy, and neither was Roy. There
was debate as to what to do next. It finally reached an impasse, resulting in
Roy withholding the publishing rights. This basically scuppered the project,
creating a toxic relationship between the parties.

Some tracks had been developed past the demo stage, and even the album
cover had been designed when the plug was pulled. It looked like it might be the
end of the road for Roy and EMI. Roy had used Black Sheep to quickly record a
rough version of the album. Although there were three or four excellent tracks,
there was no epic amongst them; the album lacked bite, being out of step with
the new punk ethos. Roy felt he would've produced more viable material had he
been allowed to record with the quality and stability of Abbey Road Studios.

The name *Commercial Breaks (Doesn't it?),* probably sums it up. The album
lacked the gravitas of its immediate predecessors, in the wake of which it
was definitely a lightweight. Perhaps the project was too rushed. Or maybe it
was an attempt to do precisely what EMI had wanted: to produce something
commercial that would make money. The irony!

In the meantime, Pete Jenner had become involved with Ian Dury, making Jenner unavailable to work with Roy. Jenner turning up occasionally was not enough to improve the album; perhaps he was the missing ingredient.

Whatever the reason, *Commercial Breaks (Doesn't it?)* didn't equal Roy's previous albums: being neither an artistic success nor a viable commercial enterprise, despite its title's implication. Roy described it as a set of demos: 'For me, they'll always represent strings of unfinished and abandoned ideas'.

The tracks were not released until 1988 after Roy had secured control of all his EMI work. The bulk of the tracks were first released on the Awareness label's 1988 album, *Loony On The Bus*. In 1994, the full album was finally issued in its original (unfinished) form, on CD through Roy's own Science Friction label.

'My Little Girl'
This song starts the album at a jaunty pace with full pop treatment. There is a band, female backing vocals and a catchy chorus. But in the end, it's just a pop song of no great consequence.

'I'm In Love With You'
'I'm In Love With You' begins with a steady drum beat, bass and strummed guitars. Like Roy's other love songs, the vocal delivery is soft and gentle. As the chorus approaches, the organ and backing intensify, creating a fuller sound. The song has potential but doesn't quite succeed. With the right production and instrumentation, it could've been so much more: as indeed was proven later when it was re-recorded for the *Unknown Soldier* album, where the addition of the David Bedford strings really improved the track.

'Ten Years Ago'
This is a much heavier track, more in the style of *HQ*, and based on a great riff. Roy is reacting to the exploding punk scene that usurped the old guard. Even Roy – the archetypal rebel – felt labelled as past-it: the punks and critics perceiving him as being part of 'the system'. Ten years earlier, he was the crazy rebel who dreamed of a better world, of overthrowing the establishment or at least creating a culture that was completely apart from it. Now, the world, and society, was still the same; the rebellion had made no difference; the environment was still plundered, and the establishment still ran the place. Bureaucracy proliferated, creating pointless work. Nothing changes.

Interestingly, John Lydon (Johnny Rotten of Sex Pistols) once said that the best advantage of being courted by EMI was the opportunity to help himself to freebie albums. He grabbed the Roy Harper records, so not all the new wave of rebels saw Roy as superfluous.

'Sail Away'
After the punchy 'Ten Years Ago' comes a complete contrast: a wistful ballad with guitar, bass, drums, a chorus of ethereal organ and dreamy harmonies.

Despite the change of mood, the theme continues: Roy points out that all rebellion ends in failure, but we should keep striving to create change. While new rebels talk of the dawn of a new age – pointing accusingly at the 1960s failures – they merely cling to their dreams by their fingertips. They, too, will taste failure. We are all being hung out to dry.

This was released as a single, in anticipation of the album that never happened.

'I Wanna Be Part Of The News'
Here we have a fast rhythm with bubbling bass, overlaid with guitars, getting busier and louder as it progresses. I enjoy the Egyptian flourish in the last verse.

The lyrics address the emerging celebrity culture that was taking hold at the time. People were doing whatever they could to be photographed, to make the news, to be seen and mentioned. Many wanted to be important and famous, regardless of talent or substance. This culture has become much worse since the song was written.

'Cora'
Side two begins with a love song to Cora Hendriquez: a girl Roy met in Cuba in 1967. Roy's manager, Joe Lustig, secured a 'cultural' gig there for Roy and singer/songwriter Julie Felix. It boggles the mind to think what the Cubans made of Roy. He was eager to learn more about the revolution (a topic that would recur in 'Same Shoes'). He spent hours talking to Cora and never forgot her.

'Come Up And See Me'
Another love song – this time about Verna (the mother of Roy's son Ben), and is based on a calling card she passed to Roy when they first met. It's a tender song, with great drums from the 'Admiral' and organ from Dave Lawson. The guitar that kicks in the chorus creates a memorable refrain. Good, but not one of his best.

'The Fly Catcher'
This is the album's most outstanding track. After leaving Kilburn, Roy, Mocy and Nick moved to an idyllic Lavender Cottage in Wiltshire. It had a garden full of trees and a large bird population. The flycatcher was a regular visitor to a huge cherry tree. On winter evenings, the family would roast chestnuts on the log burner. There were local tales of a ghostly carriage that would gallop across the hills on moonlit nights. Roy put it all together in this love song for Mocy.

The song has a beautiful melody, which Roy sings with a gentle wistfulness. He is ably supported by drums much to the fore, atmospheric piano and some great electric guitar. This should have been a single.

'Too Many Movies'

An electric guitar proceeds into a plodding dirge-like rhythm which actually creates an interesting tension.

The song is a real dig at Nancy: Roy's American girlfriend in the early 70s. She had left him, taking their one-year-old son with her. The lyrics – packed with many contemporary film references – clearly reflect Roy's emotional state. The parallel theme is that of Caryl Chessman, who spent twelve years on death row for rape, robbery and abduction, before being cruelly and controversially executed.

Roy says there never was a good version of this song, and if the album was ever re-released, he'd leave it out. I can understand that: it is intensely emotional, with bitterness verging on the vindictive. The hurt shows and the vitriol is gushing. In my opinion, that doesn't stop it from being an excellent song and this great version is an album highlight. The live version on The BBC Tapes Vol III (also on the bootleg, Heavy Crazy) is also good.

'Square Boxes'

A quirky experimental number. The vocal is rather submerged in the chirpy guitar riff, leading to a chorus that is quite chilling. The phrase 'Happy days are here again', smacks of Aldous Huxley's happy drug, soma, from his Brave New World novel. Then there is a Big Brother mention, straight out of George Orwell's 1984 nightmare. We all go home to our square boxes to watch our square boxes. Society is firmly pacified and controlled.

Then there's the song's chaotic, mad ending! It's all a bit crazy, harking back to 'Committed' on the first album.

Extra Tracks for the 1994 CD release on the Science Friction label
'Burn The World (Part 1)'

Taken from *Loony On The Bus*, this experimental song is a precursor to the longer 'Burn The World' from 1990. Roy plays guitar, singing with a strained, anguished vocal, entirely appropriate to the subject matter. We are in the process of destroying the planet. Perhaps, in one fell swoop, we shall burn all life from the planet in a nuclear holocaust. The lyrics and their delivery seem to suggest this will be the inevitable outcome. There is a religious fervour: 'I am the light, I am the way'. Out of the mindless confusion of society, we will destroy.

The guitar paints ominous tones as the vocal applies agonising splashes of colour to the envisaged horrific future. We shall destroy ourselves and everything else. We will burn the world. You can feel the torment in Roy's voice. The powerful climax tears at you. Who else could write a song like this?

'Playing Prisons'

Another track taken from *Loony On The Bus*. It's a basic production with electrified acoustic guitar, a little whistling and an organ near the end for added effect. The stark song describes a bitter lover's accusations, as Roy reflects on his past and the many times he has ended relationships and walked away from his children, seeking rainbows with a 'grass is greener' attitude. The relationship becomes the prison, and Roy does not want to be trapped. Yet, perhaps, he takes the prison with him?

I'm not really sure why these two tracks were tagged on here. If filler was required, a live version of one or two album songs might've been more appropriate.

The Unknown Soldier (1980)

First released on the Harvest label in 1980
Personnel:
Pete Jenner/Roy Harper: producer
Roy Harper: vocals, guitar and songwriting
Kate Bush: vocals on 'You (The Games Part II)'
Dave Gilmour: guitar and songwriting on 'Playing Games', 'You (The Games Part II)', 'Old Faces', 'Short And Sweet', 'True Story'.
Andy Roberts: guitar
Steve Broughton: guitar
Hugh Burns: guitar
Sal DiTroia: guitar
B. J. Cole: steel guitar
Tony Levin: bass
Jimmy Bain: bass
Will Lee: bass
David Lawson: keyboards
Pete Wingfield: keyboards
Don Grolnick: keyboards
Jimmy Maelen: percussion
Andy Newmark: percussion
Other musicians:
George Constantino
Jim Cuomo
Timmy Donald
Neil Jason
Joe Partridge
Sara Pozzo
Dave Scance
David Bedford: orchestrations
Recorded at Abbey Road, House of Music – West Orange (New Jersey), Aquarium Studio (Paris), Chapel Lane Studio (Hereford) and Rockfield studios (Monmouth)
Roy Harper: photos and cover design

The wounds had healed a little after the *Commercial Breaks* debacle, and Roy was back in (semi) favour with EMI. They were giving him one more chance to come up with the goods, and he was giving them a fling. Though till not fully based at Abbey Road, at least he had producer, Pete Jenner, back again. They made a formidable team.

Unfortunately, Black Sheep had not survived as a band, although Andy Roberts and Dave Lawson were still around. Roy had come to terms with the fact that he was no longer on the EMI A-list, but he had the *Commercial Breaks* songs to work with, plus a new batch of five Dave Gilmour co-writes (Roy on lyrics): 'Playing Games', 'You (The Game Part II)', 'Old Faces', 'Short And Sweet' and 'True Story').

Dave Gilmour played guitar on a number of tracks, and Kate Bush – who was a huge Roy fan – agreed to sing on 'You (The Game Part II)'.

Things were looking good. Roy had a vivid concept for the album cover. He headed for France and the World War I battlefields of Verdun to take photos, and of course, despair at the terrible loss of life.

The album had no epics, but with some outstanding tracks and the involvement of Bush and Gilmour, there was a chance of success. The mood was positive, with everyone hoping for the proverbial breakthrough. But with the changing times, the music press was very much in the hands of the new wave of writers for whom figures like Dave Gilmour and Roy Harper were viewed with disdain. The album was unfairly slated and – with no help from EMI's luke-warm promotion – once again, a Harper album failed to gain the recognition it deserved.

'Playing Games' (Harper, Gilmour)

Starting with a pop song – no matter how good it was – seemed an unwise decision. Roy needed this album to be taken seriously. The opener was not indicative of the rest of the album. There is an attempt to sound modern, with more emphasis on the organ and synthesizer, instead of the standard guitar format. It does have a catchy chorus and might well have attracted some airplay, but maybe not with the audience that Roy really wanted. There is a lot going for the track, though: the band is good, there is some great guitar, and it's well-produced.

The lyric concerns the serious subject of the bickering and games that can occur during a relationship disintegration. It describes the arguing, threats and introspection that take place in the attempts to force a reaction and hurt each other.

With a different treatment, the track might have worked well, but this pop arrangement doesn't do it for me. I can see why it did not appeal to the rebellious press critics. This is a long way from rebel Roy Harper and even further from punk.

'I'm In Love With You'

One of the tracks salvaged from *Commercial Breaks*. The original version was more basic. This re-recording is softer, with gentler tones and more instrumentation: a production that suits the song's mood. The David Bedford string arrangement adds to the emotion and feel. Roy has taken the original, re-analysed it and created something superior, making it one of his best love songs.

'The Fly Catcher'

Another re-recording of a *Commercial Breaks* song. The original version was very good, but this is tighter and has more impact. Once again, the strings add to the atmosphere. The vocal is more immediate and the guitar break is powerful, soaring to emotional heights.

'You (The Game Part II)' (Harper, Gilmour)

Roy wanted to duet with a female singer. He had successfully done so a number of times, the first being with Jane Scrivener on *Folkjokeopus*. A duet with Kate Bush was exactly what he envisaged for this song.

Dave Gilmour had been a long-time friend of Roy's, having previously worked together on Dave's solo track, 'Short And Sweet', and Dave had contributed to previous Harper albums. This project took their collaboration to a new level. Dave had been instrumental in launching Kate Bush's career, and Kate was a Roy fan, so when a female voice was needed, there was a mutual desire to work together. The end result was bound to be something exceptional.

'You (The Game Part II)' is about sex and the magic DNA molecule whose double helix and codes create the vast array of life on the planet; it's about the human desire and attraction that results in sexual procreation. Kate opens the song in a seductive tone. Roy responds directly, the two combining in sublime harmony for the chorus. Dave's guitar drives with power in true Floydian style.

This works so well on every level. It's such a shame it didn't open the album.

'Old Faces' (Harper, Gilmour)

Another track Dave Gilmour's music and Roy's words. There is an atmosphere of nostalgia as Roy wistfully reminisces on gatherings with old friends, sharing spliffs and discussing ideas. The atmosphere is as swirly, dreamy and laid-back.

This track came in for heavy criticism. It was referred to as 'Old Faeces': a snarly new music press barb, predictable in its response as a knee-jerk reaction to anything deemed to be smacking of the 1960s. The idea being that if it wasn't punk, it wasn't worth anything. They had no time for dreamy nostalgia. Shame.

'Short And Sweet' (Harper, Gilmour)

This is Roy's version of he and Gilmour's collaboration from the latter's eponymous 1978 solo album. It is interesting to compare the two versions – both equally brilliant. Strangely, Dave does not appear on this recording. He wrote the chords, but they are delivered by the great Andy Roberts.

The track is a truly magnificent beast, not only for the superb guitar and heavy power chords – but listen to that bass. The backing really does justice the incredible lyric and vocal delivery.

The poem itself is not easily explained. It needs to be mulled over. What is this life that we are leading? How should we be living it? What is the quality of life? Can we find fellow travellers, friends, who share our vision? Is it worth striving for something better? What is this great society we are part of, and how does it impinge on our lives and our freedoms? What is morality? Can we – despite the claustrophobia of control – be free in our minds to carve a worthy life together? So many questions. So much to think about. The song carries some heavy philosophy, worthy of far greater consideration than the critics gave it.

The song later appeared on the live tape, *Born In Captivity II*. Delivered solo, it is a powerful, superb version, though, for some reason, it was omitted from the CD issue: titled 'Unhinged'.

'First Thing In The Morning'
The synthesizer and drum pattern create an easy-listening feel, with a catchy chorus and buzzy/jangly arrangement. The production is breezy and light considering the opening verses' sentiments, concerned as they are with the wanton mass murder of thousands of young men in order to preserve the glory of an already fading empire.

The later verses, about the superficiality of life, better fit the music's tone. Here in the aftermath, in the great new society, the new world that was fought for, we are living in our hutches, watching soaps and celebrities on the box. First thing in the morning – there's nothing to be done about it now, so snuggle up and let's make love!

'The Unknown Soldier'
Not quite as clean a production as *Flat Baroque And Berserk*. This has a busier backing, with the direct vocal very much to the fore.

It's an anti-war song with a difference, about an unimaginable and dreadful future. Roy is in the gutter, discarded, like many of our soldiers. The lyric explores the inevitability of future war, as aggressive and belligerent societies spread out across the galaxy with increasingly more terrible weapons.

Having lived through the cold war, it is easy to imagine the reality of fingers poised to press buttons that activate satellites and unleash doomsday. It's all too real.

'Ten Years Ago'
The last song salvaged from the aborted *Commercial Breaks* album. This re-recording takes a different production route to the original. Instead of the heavy guitar, it starts with a fabulous bass that persists throughout the track. The guitar comes in later; the production has a more modern feel, and the backing, busier. I wouldn't say it is necessarily better – just different.

'True Story' (Harper, Gilmour)
The album ends with the last of the Harper/Gilmour collaborations. It begins with a doom-laden synthesizer; bass, drums and guitar then setting up a fast pace. The image of a medieval army galloping to war comes to mind, with the hooves of those great chargers thundering into battle. Dave created a pulsating, furious track towards which Roy pitched his poetic and graphic labs of history. Roy being a history buff, this is his musical interpretation of some gory events.

It starts with the battle of Bannockburn. The second part concerns the horrendous murder of the homosexual King, Edward the Second. He was held down on the bed with a heavy oak table while red hot pokers were thrust up his anus. His screams woke people in nearby villages. When people saw his body the next day, his grotesque, anguished face belied the story that he had died in his sleep. The third section is about Henry de Bohun, who charged Robert the Bruce, the day before the battle of Bannockburn. Bruce evaded his charge, splitting Henry's head clean in two with one stroke of his sword.

Gilmour's music is the perfect background for Roy's storytelling. The grand production has many sound effects, and you can imagine Roy and Dave having great fun putting this together. Rarely have episodes in our gory history been so well illustrated in song.

All told, *The Unknown Soldier* is an album of distinction, with a number of worthy tracks that deserved a greater response from both critics and the public.

Singles

Two singles were released to promote the album.

'Playing Games' b/w 'First Thing In The Morning'

'Playing Games' was chosen as a single, obviously because of its jaunty pop feel, and the possibility it might be a chart contender. Neither track was really representative of the album, nor were they among its strongest numbers. But then, the charts are not about quality are they? They are about mass appeal.

'Short And Sweet' b/w 'Watersports' (Live)/'Unknown Soldier' (Live)

This A-side was c ertainly one of the album's strongest songs, and was probably too good for the pop charts.

'Watersports' has never been released anywhere else: not really surprising, as it is not so much a song as an amusing tale of urination. This is Roy at his most playful and outrageous – really pushing the envelope.

The live version of 'Unknown Soldier' is an excellent acoustic solo rendition.

Born In Captivity (1984)

First released on the Hardup Public label 1984
Personnel:
Roy Harper: producer
Roy Harper: guitar, vocals and all songwriting
Recorded at home
Cover art and design: Roy Harper
A vinyl release of 882 copies
Re-released on Awareness records (1985) and then on Science Friction (1989) as
CDs and tapes

I have included this 1984 album before 1982's *Work Of Heart*, as these largely
acoustic demos were made for that album. They were subsequently released
as a special collector's album in order to raise capital after the *Work Of Heart*
release. I have gone with the recording sequence rather than the release date.

Following the commercial failure of Unknown Soldier and its singles, EMI
decided to let Roy go. The decade-long relationship had produced amazing
albums but failed to yield the success Roy deserved. That was due partly to
Roy's maverick nature and his habit of shooting himself in the foot whenever
it looked like things were coming together, and partly to EMI's failure to back
him at the right time, fulfil their promises and not making marketing blunders.
Also, the nature of the material was not necessarily suited to mainstream radio
or the average punter. The music was artistically brilliant but required listening
and absorbing, not treating lightly, and Roy was not good at producing singles
– most of his pop song attempts being below par.

The EMI split was a rude shock for Roy. It came at a difficult period for him.
Suddenly he was without a label, his relationship with Verna was melting
down, the wonderful Vauld Farm was gone (repossessed by the bank), and he
found himself in severe financial trouble. However, Roy was undeterred. He set
up his own label – Public Records – and toured like mad to bring in money to
finance his new venture. He wrote songs and recorded demos for the album
that would become *Work Of Heart*. The songs were raw and stripped down to
their essence: just Roy, his acoustic guitars and a tape machine.

The album cover illustrates Roy's then beleaguered mental state. It shows
him behind bars, looking surly and defiant. The numbers 120641 represent
his date of birth; and 006: the Patrick McGoohan TV series, *The Prisoner*, that
inspired 'McGoohan's Blues'.

This was the start of a new age. Roy had to alter the way he worked, go back
to basics and manage on his own. It was only after the *Work Of Heart* release
that Roy thought of issuing the demos.

'Stan'

Roy is passionate about sport and might well have been a sportsman if he
hadn't been a musician. Cricket is his major passion, with football close

behind, Manchester City being his team. Just as he had recorded 'When An Old Cricketer Leaves The Crease', he now wrote a football song: 'Stan'.

As a boy, Roy had been fortunate to see some of the all-time greats, like Stanley Matthews and Stanley Mortenson. Saturday afternoons were for football. Roy regularly went to watch Blackpool FC with his father. Before the advent of Sky Sports, matches kicked off at 3 p.m. Passions ran high; the excitement was palpable. Sport is the replacement for hunting and war. Nothing stirs the passions quite the same, and Roy nails these feelings.

Stan is a delightful tune that captures the thrill of those Saturdays; the expectation and excitement as the match approached. As with 'One Of Those Days In England', 'Stan' captures a moment in time now long gone and part of history.

While not in quite the same league as 'When An Old Cricketer Leaves The Crease' (lacking the metaphorical dimension that gives 'Cricketer' another level), it does succeed in capturing the emotion of the time. It's a shame Roy did not record 'Stan' for the album. It would have been interesting to see how it might have developed with more production. The potential is there.

'Drawn To The Flames'

This poem contains much philosophy. Roy sings about being alive on this planet, loose in nature, spinning through the stars in a metaphysical state of being, 'Despite the trials and tribulations', daring to live and take risks, until the end of the game. He is espousing his anarchic philosophy.

The first two verses are a love song, with the chorus foretelling our end. Are we – like many other creatures – drawn to the light?; 'Drawn to the flames' to burn ourselves out? He is saying how here on this 'water world', we could dare to give up everything, take up a simpler life, return to nature, and be completely free.

'Come To Bed Eyes'

This is a love song about the mutual attraction when two people connect: catching each other's eyes across a room full of people. For Roy as a musician on stage, this can happen often, but it could be anyone anywhere. The chemistry of attraction floods the mind with an urgent longing to be together, yet there are often many obstacles. Will it ever happen? Could it ever happen? Please find a way.

'No Woman Is Safe'

The guitars tuned to DADGAD here combine to create another lilting love song. Here, it is played in a higher key than on *Work of Heart*. The chords are sensitive, communicating sadness and yearning. By the end, the vocal rises to the level of anguished pain. With the end of another relationship, there is a longing to find a soulmate, someone to help Roy survive the nightmare of society and fulfil his dreams. She must be out there waiting. When they meet, he will steal her heart. He is the 'Jack of Hearts', and she, the perfect queen.

It's an idealised romantic song, born from the endless search for perfection.

'I Am A Child'

'I Am A Child' creates a late-night jazz vibe. Despite the drums, electric guitar and keyboards, the feel is perhaps too understated. The lyrics are also rather downbeat: the constant battle of the day, the need to leave reality behind, to run away into dreams, to be free, to escape with a spliff, to look towards better days of love and music, heading for a new land where everything is right. It has a desperate edge. One of Roy's boasts used to be that he breaks the law every day: whether by exceeding the speed limit or smoking a joint.

'Elizabeth'

The guitars chime brightly, deploying strong Major 7ths, as with 'When An Old Cricketer Leaves The Crease' and 'Twelve Hours Of Sunset'. Although the song is rather dirge-like, the chords are uplifting. It's a beautiful love song with a haunting melody.

For the song's first part, Verna (middle name Elizabeth) returns to America, Roy dwelling on the failed relationship, before opening up into a global perspective. 'It's time we come together to make things better' is his plea to Verna and everyone. It's time to join together, no matter what our differences; time to protest, to make a better world and save the planet. Time – before it's over. But the lyrics do display optimism: there is a way forward – 'a room with a view'.

'Work Of Heart'

This is the album's main event: a 19-minute epic with six distinct movements. Even though music was veering away from the long sophisticated canvas to short, punchier numbers, Roy chose to buck the trend completely.

Although this doesn't quite measure up to the brilliance of 'The Lord's Prayer' or 'McGoohan's Blues', 'Work Of Heart' is still a monster of a song. Parts of the construction take me back to *Stormcock*. In defiance of commerciality, Roy is again reaching for something more substantial; an artistic statement in music and words. This opus intricately weaves many moods and contains a poem of deep meaning. It takes the large canvas of human civilisation, the terrible state of our greed-ridden society; the absurdity of believing that we can leave this planet for some afterlife, and states that love within a perfect relationship is the only escape.

In this stipped-bare version, Roy shows his full vocal range and ability to marry intricate progressions and melodies to his poetry in compelling ways.

I. 'No One Gets Out Alive'

Right from the opening punctuating chords (reminiscent of 'Short And Sweet'), we know we are in for a ride. It leads straight into what acts as a chorus:

'No one ever gets out alive'. There is no afterlife. This is all we have. Thank heavens. Life is fleeting; 'No longer than a bee on a flower'.

II. 'Two Lovers In The Moon'
The mood now becomes more sanguine, reflecting the lyrics. There's disillusionment with the people running the world. The question is asked – living in this society run by a wealthy elite – can we find a corner for ourselves, away from this mess? Roy will take his woman and look for somewhere else, even if it's only for a stolen moment.

III. 'We Are The People'
There's a change to a faster rhythm as the vocal rises, the song sliding into a section reminiscent of 'Me And My Woman'. Roy suggests that we do not have time to dwell on all this slime. We only have each other. But maybe, we, the people, could change it.

IV. 'All Us Children (So Sadly Far Apart)'
The music shifts into a softer mode. Roy entreats his love to join him in search of a better life and asks for 'all us children' spread so far apart to share this vision.

V. 'We Are The People (Reprise)'
The resuming riff heralds the return of the 'We Are The People' chorus. Roy introduces an element of hope: despite the terrible controlling forces around us, we could still join, to forge a better life.

VI. 'No One Ever Gets Out Alive (Finale)'
The final section resurrects those punctuating chords and that hypnotic chorus. Roy states that this life is all we have. We have to make the most of it because we are not going anywhere else.

Work Of Heart (1982)

First released on the Public label in 1982
Personnel:
Roy Harper/David Lord: producers
M. E. Thompson: executive producer
Roy Harper: vocals, electric and acoustic guitar, synthesiser and songwriting
Bob Wilson: electric and acoustic guitars
Tony Franklyn: electric bass, fretless bass and percussion
David Morris: piano, synthesiser, clarinet, pizzicato viola
Charlie Morgan: drums
Dick Morrisey: saxophone
Daniel Lockhart: drums on 'Woman' and 'I Am A Child'
Dorian Healey: additional drums
Paul Cobbold: additional bass, engineer
Dave Morgan: Oberheim DMX drum computer programmes
David Lord: tubular bells and additional synthesisers, engineer
Yvonne D'Cruz: additional vocal on 'Woman'
The Harpies (Bob Wilson, Tony Franklyn, John David): backing vocals
John Leckie: engineer
Tom Oliver: engineer
Recorded at Chapel Lane Studio
Cover design: Roy Harper/Jacqui Turner

After falling in love again (with Jacqui), Roy started writing and recording new songs. He gathered together some excellent musicians, the nucleus of which made up the touring band used to promote the album. He also teamed up with Mark Thompson (son of historian and CND activist, E. P. Thompson) to set up a label: Public Records.

Taking the new demos (later to be released as the above-outlined *Born In Captivity*), Roy set up in Hereford's Chapel Lane Studio and began honing them into a more sophisticated form. He was familiar with the studio, having worked there during the recording of Unknown Soldier. It lacked the quality of Abbey Road but shared some aspects, and the results were very pleasing. But the employed multi-layering approach of albums like *Stormcock* and *Bullinamingvase*, made *Work Of Heart* sound overproduced. Despite winning awards, the album was criticised, many fans preferring the later-released *Born In Captivity* demos. Roy was striving for a modern sound: based less on guitars and more on synthesizers – something progressive rock reflected in the late 1970s.

Some of the demos were developed no further: neither 'Stan' nor 'Come To Bed Eyes' made it onto the album. 'No Woman Is Safe' – left virtually unchanged – was renamed 'Jack Of Hearts'. Two new tracks also appeared: 'Woman' and 'I Still Care'. The end result was an excellent, substantial album of progressive rock and poetic lyrics, even if the synthesizers do date it to that particular period.

Interestingly, *Work Of Heart* was very well-received by critics (unlike *The Unknown Soldier),* and Derek Jewel of the *Sunday Times* even chose it as Record Of The Year.

'Drawn To The Flames'

It is amazing to hear how this basic song – as heard on *Born In Captivity* – was worked into this sophisticated and powerful track. The band is in full swing, with a welling of synthesizers, guitars, drums and bass, creating a rich sound augmented by backing vocals and effects. There is a saxophone solo, and a piano creates tinkling water sounds. Roy's vocal is confident and commanding. It's a great start to the album, but I'm not sure which version I prefer.

'Jack Of Hearts'

Starting life as 'No Woman Is Safe', this new version has a bright, vibrant production based around Roy's warm, rich acoustic guitar sound. There is a more poppy vibe than on the demo, which leaves me with mixed feelings.

'I Am A Child'

A rather plodding song on *Born In Captivity,* this production is quite a transformation. It still has that jazz feel but is much more interesting. There's a lot going on, and I love that drum rhythm being nicely to the fore. But it's still very laid-back with a spliffed-out feel.

'Woman'

This was one of the new songs. Roy had an ongoing battle with the women's liberation movement. There was something about it that he disapproved of, yet he has always expressed ideals of equality. This unease extends back to the *Come Out Fighting Ghengis Smith* track, 'All You Need Is', and the *Valentine* tracks, 'Male Chauvinist Pig Blues' and 'Magic Woman (Liberation Reshuffle)'. I detect ambivalence. Roy likes the idea of equality and freedom but perhaps sees it in sexual terms.

The lyric expresses a wish for equality in romantic relationship. It is interesting to note the female chorus near the end, referring back to a line from Patrick McGoohan's The Prisoner: 'I am not a number, I am a free woman'. Roy here changed man for woman.

Roy here went for a more modern production, with a weird organ-based intro heralding a spacey guitar feel. Once again, drums are to the fore, the vibe maintained through light echoey guitars, though the chorus is a bit punchier.

Roy claims the song to be a dismal failure.

'I Still Care'

This, the second of the new tracks, is a love song with a difference. The title says it all. Roy's relationship with Verna was falling apart after much disagreement. The love they had was deep, but there was that old chestnut of control. Verna wanted Roy to change, and he resisted. He couldn't and he wouldn't. They kept breaking up. They drove each other crazy, although deep down, he still loved her. If only they could find their way back to the smiles and love. The song is a direct plea to Verna.

It starts with swirling synthesisers, creating a plaintive feel. The vocal has an anguished, emotional tone. Coming in on the chorus, the band bring a warmer sound, raising the mood before it's back to the synthesizers and emotive vocal.

As a song, it works well. As a plea for reconciliation, it failed miserably.

'Work Of Heart'
I. No One Gets Out Alive
This starts with the same punctuating chords as the demo, though less strident due to the underlying drums and synthesizers. Roy's voice is in top form. Backing vocals augment the chorus as it builds into a powerful guitar-based riff. The drums are again mixed to the fore. The powerful saxophone solo adds an interesting element. The section comes to a halt, pausing before the next part.

II. 'Two Lovers In The Moon'
The mood changes, the music slows. The vocal is whimsical, with an underlying synthesizer and soft guitars. The drums come in, the music building to a steady pace with stronger vocal, climaxing in swirling synthesizers and a rising set of vocal harmonies.

III. 'We Are The People'
The guitar riff cuts in with Roy focussing on the lower strings. The pace is more intense, his voice mirroring that. The band is full-on – the chorus creates a high note with call and response.

IV. 'All Us Children (So Sadly Far Apart)'
The backing drops out, leaving just the vocal and synthesizers. The guitars return with a refrain, culminating in drums and percussion, Roy's voice echoing. The electric guitar becomes acoustic guitar, the voice now in a high register. The bass weaves patterns behind the guitar, creating a soft, melodic section.

V. 'We Are The People (Reprise)'
Guitar and drums lead the band to the reprise. The riff returns as Roy delivers the final verse.

VI. 'No One Ever Gets Out Alive (Finale)'
The finale is a reprise of 'No One Ever Gets Out Alive', building to a full band climax.

Singles
'No One Ever Gets Out Alive' b/w 'Casualty' (Live at Glastonbury)

The A-side is a section taken from the album track, 'Work Of Heart'.

'Casualty' eventually appeared in a studio-recorded version on the 1988 album, *Loony On The Bus*. After twenty years of showbiz life, failed relationships and living outside the law, Roy is the casualty: though often through his own making. But at live gigs, it was a standard piece of music hall entertainment, with Roy looning it up, sometimes spraying digestive biscuit crumbs from his mouth. This live version came from Glastonbury 1982, with The Roy Harper Band consisting of Bob Wilson, Tony Franklin, Dave Morris and George Jackson. The funky sound was not too dissimilar to Ian Dury and the Blockheads. The band is tight, the bass picking out great runs while the organ keeps up a steady pulsating beat. The drums pound and the guitar takes a back seat. This gives Roy the perfect base to perform his best *Monty Python*. It all culminates in a truly crazy bit of fun. The song invariably provided a light-hearted interlude at shows and was a real crowd-pleaser.

'I Still Care' b/w 'Goodbye Ladybird' (Acoustic)

'I Still Care' was rather a strange choice for a single. It is a delightful song but was really too intense for chart success.

'Goodbye Ladybird' was another song about the end of a relationship. Roy did not rate this track very highly, but it is a pleasant enough song with some enjoyable guitar and a gentle melody. It could easily have been the A-side. It has a certain charm, if not much substance.

Whatever Happened To Jugula? (1985) Roy Harper and Jimmy Page

First released on the Beggars Banquet label in 1985
Personnel:
Roy Harper: producer
Roy Harper: vocals, acoustic and electric guitars, percussion and all songwriting
Jimmy Page: acoustic and electric guitars
Nick Harper: semi-acoustic guitar
Tony Franklin: bass guitar
Nik Green: keyboards, engineer
Ronnie Brambles: drums
Steve Broughton: drums
Preston Heyman: drums
Recorded at Clapham, Hereford, Berkshire, Mamaraneck West Cork, and Boilerhouse studios, Lytham.
Koala Bear: artwork and cover design
Highest UK chart place: 44

Without a label, Roy was in a wilderness. Public Records – the label he set up with Mark Thompson – had folded. Running the label had proven to be time-consuming and expensive. Additionally, keeping the band together became impossible: the band ran at a loss, even when touring, and without an album to promote, it simply wasn't viable. Tony Franklin later went off to work with Jimmy Page's new band, The Firm.

Tony Beck – an old school friend of Roy's from Lytham – provided the studio where most of *Whatever Happened To Jugula?* was recorded. Tony suggested Roy renew his friendship with Jimmy Page and bring him on board for the album. Jimmy agreed, providing a lifeline that enabled Roy to secure a recording contract on the indie label, Beggars Banquet. Most of the recording occurred at Jimmy's house, on an eight-track TEAC reel-to-reel machine on loan from Pete Townshend.

For a while, the album's working title was *Rizla* (after the papers used for rolling joints). Then it was going to be *Whatever Happened To Harper and Page*? But Roy considered that cashing in on Jimmy's name too much. Then it became *What Ever Happened To 1214*? (the year the Magna Carta was signed), but that was considered too obscure. Finally, one night Roy and Jimmy were playing Trivial Pursuit. Roy had a thing about saying 'go for the jugula', so the album title was born. It was just a matter of design firm, Koala Bear, adding 'Jugula?' to the partially completed cover artwork. Some people actually bought two copies, so they could cut one cover up into a giant Rizla. Perhaps going a little too far??

From the start, this had been a Roy Harper album with Jimmy Page contributions (as opposed to a true collaboration). All the songs were Roy's (apart from the Harper/Gilmour composition, 'Hope'), and Jimmy simply added guitar. The venture brought fresh life to Roy's career, and the album actually made the charts. This led to Roy being re-signed to EMI, giving him more security and a new lease of life. Hats off to Jimmy Page.

Jimmy's involvement did not stop at working on the album: he also took part in promotion, appearing with Roy on *The Old Grey Whistle Test*. They also went on the road for some promotional gigs, including the Cambridge Folk Festival. But in a less-than-satisfactory interview in the Lake District hills, Mark Ellen rather disparagingly portrayed the pair as 1970s rock dinosaurs. But the interview did showcase acoustic versions of 'Hangman' and 'Same Old Rock'.

As for the album? Despite Page's presence, it did not sell well and failed to secure great reviews, although it did make the top 50. Roy's name was perhaps still a little toxic to the music press, but reaching the UK charts was a major breakthrough.

The production was bright and clear. It is much more guitar-orientated – as one would imagine with Jimmy Page in the fold – but there was still room for some keyboards and effects.

'Nineteen Forty-Eightish'

During 1984, Roy had the idea of writing a song to commemorate the George Orwell novel 1984. Written in 1948, Orwell had simply turned the numbers around. The oppressive, controlled state Orwell envisaged was now obvious in a number of ways. This idea of state control is a theme that has preoccupied Roy for most of his life and is anathema to him.

The track, at just short of ten minutes, is the album's epic. Verse one is a dystopian vision: a description of the relentless, pointless drudgery of society's bureaucracy. Roy hates it so much that he would prefer to wipe it out altogether by pressing that button.

The album begins with Roy singing in despair at our stupidity over a lush synth strings sound. The second section is guitar-based: Jimmy's restrained phrases cutting into the song. Roy despairs over us, drowning in a flood of paper, bills and rubbish that take up so much of our precious time, stopping us from living. The lyric even mentions the time they are rolling a joint as the authorities break in. There is a parallel theme of King Alfred – whose problems distracted him so much that he allowed the cakes to burn.

In the third section, the electric guitar underpins the acoustic, as Roy and Jimmy spar. The last section features both players on acoustic: Roy's unique rich tone coming from his Ovation semi-acoustic.

Roy's wonderful vocal harmonies seem in contrast to the song's dire message. He is distraught. The nightmare of control is all-pervasive. Society seeks to regulate our every move. Our schools peddle the establishment message. The whole crazy, polluted system perpetuates itself, heading towards destruction. The only possible escape is an absurd afterlife conjured up through desperation.

The nightmare is the life he's living. It's 1984, and it's real.

81

'Bad Speech'

In a complete change of pace, 'Bad Speech' is a poem given a similar
treatment to the poem that began 'The Lord's Prayer'. There is no backing
to speak of, apart from occasional synthesizer, whistling, and wafting
background vocals to create interest. The words and their delivery alone are
sufficient.

The poem – just over one minute in length – deals with humanity, the
struggle of evolution, the pathetic direction society has taken, and disbelief
in God. It lauds the planet that gives us life but foresees its demise when it
is consumed, as our sun explodes to become a red giant. The poem merges
with the next track, which seems appropriate. Despite everything, there is
always hope.

'Hope' (Roy Harper/Dave Gilmour)

Originally, Dave Gilmour sent a copy of this music to both Roy, and Pete
Townsend, in the hope that one of them might come up with a lyric so he
could include the song on his second solo album. Pete came up with 'White
City Fighting', and Roy produced 'Hope': neither of which Dave could relate to
enough to use.

Roy adapted 'Hope' for the album – his 16-year-old son Nick (already an
amazing guitarist) on semi-acoustic, Page on electric fills, Nick Green on
synthesizers and Tony Franklin on bass. Jimmy's part is an intricate circular
pattern that is sheer perfection in its timing. The song builds to a heavy
crescendo, then dropping away to a complete change of mood, Roy's aching
vocal above a delicate keyboard, with a bass line mimicking the melody. The
drums and guitar reappear at the chorus. It is certainly powerful, with a
memorable melody.

The lyric is poetic, as one has come to expect. It's written from the
perspective of someone in the future looking back in time and glimpsing us as
'strange archaeology', as well as being real people. Roy simultaneously peers
into the distant future, sensing the presence of those future generations. It
has a weird metaphysic. He is implying that we humans want to leave our
impression on the future; to have been known to have lived; to have helped
shape and make the world a better place: in so doing, perhaps living forever.
We live on in our DNA strands, forever tied to the planet, not as spirits flying
off to some imaginary afterlife.

'Hangman'

Here Roy and Jimmy duel on acoustic guitars, Jimmy embellishing with
bursts of lead guitar. The drums and bass have a subdued but important role,
emphasising the phrases. Jimmy's sublime, crystal-clear extended notes and
heavy chords accentuate the chorus.

The number is heartfelt, with roots in Roy's prison experience. As a young
man, he would regularly walk past the death cell where condemned prisoners

spent their last day. Such a man would be taken from the death cell to an adjoining room, where he was fitted with the noose. When the trapdoor opened, he fell, usually breaking his neck. Sometimes his head was pulled off. Sometimes he was not killed immediately, taking many long minutes to die. Bodies were buried in quicklime on unconsecrated ground. The graves were unmarked and the quicklime dissolved the remains. The only clue left to their existence was a number in the governor's office. This left a huge impact on Roy. It was an immoral process he was strongly against, so he created this graphic song to document all he felt was wrong with the process. He describes it as cold-blooded state murder. The fact that a number of innocent people were hung in error is one reason for the present-day abhorrence of capital punishment – which the UK abolished in 1965. Yet, there are some who would like to see it reinstated.

The lyric leaves nothing to the imagination. For once, the words are direct, descriptive and unambiguous.

'Elizabeth'
The *Born In Captivity* version of 'Elizabeth' is an acoustic joy. I wondered how Roy and Jimmy would tackle it with full studio production. In the first section, the guitars are crisper, the production smoother, though it is fundamentally the same. That changes at the chorus, where the band brings a full, richer sound. The chorus crescendo leads to some exquisite electric guitar that adds a further dimension. The full-bodied production provides a good contrast to the acoustic version. Both versions are well worth listening to.

'Frozen Moment'
Having heard Roy perform this live on a number of occasions, I was again intrigued again to hear how the song might be approached and what role there could possibly be for Jimmy. The song is Roy's attempt to write with just one chord.

This arrangement is very similar to the live version. Keyboards augment the acoustic guitars, with multitracked vocals at the end. A single chiming chord remains for the poem – originally written for Jacqui – to be sung over. One morning, Roy awoke, transfixed by her beauty, left in the thrall of emotional wondering. He called it a premonition – holding that perfect image in his mind and wondering at what the future might bring.

'Twentieth Century Man'
There can't be many songs that are an ode to mutual oral sex, and it is unlikely that any would be as explicit as this. Roy takes us on a journey with an orgasmic end, leaving nothing to the imagination.

Roy sets the basic acoustic guitar chords, Jimmy picking and playing around on another. They meld perfectly. You can see why they enjoy playing as a duo: two 20th century beasts on the guitar.

'Advertisement (Another Intentional Irrelevant Suicide)'

Roy obviously knew this was likely to reinforce many critics' view of him as a stoned druggie to be dismissed. From his 1950s beat poet days, he had been an advocate of hash. Nothing was going to prevent him from enjoying his spliff. Consequently, he had no compunction about producing this: another of his rather humorous, piss-takes.

The track starts with manic laughter. To guitar accompaniment, Roy staggers off in a stoned state, to the loo, to piss on his own shoe. The tone is set.

At the chorus, the band comes in: 'I'm really stoned, really stoned/ Permanently out my bone/I'm really stoned'. The rhythm thunders as the madness progresses into quite a catchy little number.

The lyric reflects a very stoned Roy who has a passing relationship with reality. It features a rather comical police officer and a farcical drug bust. A befuddled time is had by all. The song ends as it began, with more manic laughter – and Roy depositing his last meal down the toilet. There was a time when every Harper album ended with manic laughter.

I'm not sure this would get much play as a single.

12 inch Single

'Elizabeth' b/w 'Advertisement'/'I Hate The White Man' (Live)

'Elizabeth' and 'Hope' were the only two single possibilities. The inclusion of 'Advertisement' was a strange choice.

However, the live version of 'I Hate The White Man' was an interesting inclusion that would appeal to real Harper fans. That track was recorded at Poynton, Cheshire, on 18 October 1984. It is dedicated to Rosie, who was going to join Roy for the performance. But she didn't appear, and Roy sounds agitated by it: he seems angry – his guitar loud and aggressive. The recording is not pristine – his voice a little too far back – but the passion shines through nevertheless. My only criticism is that one of the verses is missing. Roy had taken to dropping a verse live, as he felt the song lost impact by being too long.

At the end, he reads the words of a Native American Crow Indian about the coming of the white man. He often read this before singing 'I Hate The White Man'. It was extremely salutary. Apart from on bootlegs, this is the only place we can hear this moving piece of writing.

Descendants Of Smith (1988)

First released on the EMI label in 1988
Personnel:
Roy Harper: producer
Jacqui Turner/Harper: sound engineer, vocals
Roy Harper: guitars, vocal and all songwriting
Stuart Elliott: drums
Tony Franklin: fretless bass
Nik Green: keyboards, piano
Nick Harper: acoustic and electric guitars, SP12 programming, vocals
Kevin McAlea: keyboards, alto saxophone
Mark Ramsden: tenor saxophone
Recorded in Roy's studio at Folkingham, Lincolnshire

By the late 1980s, Roy had begun to bring his life back into order. Being with EMI again gave him financial security. His new manager – Darren Crisp – organised an improved gigging system. Heavy traffic made getting out of London problematic. So Roy moved from Brixton to a house in Folkingham, near Spilsby, Lincolnshire. Folkingham – fairly central for accessing all parts of the country – made life easier. The house also provided the space and opportunity for Roy to set up his own studio. Life had become less fraught.

Roy had a new relationship with Jacqui Turner, who later became his wife. She was adept at the electronic side of music. Their partnership enabled Roy to develop music along different lines. With Jacqui on the mixing desk, the live gigs became electronically sophisticated, and they incorporated computer programming into the recording process. The studio in Lincolnshire was well-equipped, with Apple Macs and a state of the art mixing desk. EMI were happy for the album to be recorded there. Also, the house was large enough for people to stay and work on the album. It was all systems go.

So, in 1987 – equipped with a new set of songs, promises from EMI, a great group of musicians and confidence riding high – Roy set about creating the album he hoped would provide the second breakthrough. He had a couple of aims: to capture the experience of a live show and to adopt a more modern sound. The production and instrumentation employed on Prince's *Sign O' The Times* album had impressed Roy. As a result, *Descendants Of Smith* is interesting, with variety but no common theme. There are some excellent songs, but the album lacks cohesion. Even so, Roy had high hopes for it.

But things did not go as planned. Roy had the feeling that the music press prevented him from receiving the publicity or positive reviews he needed in order to sell records. So he and the EMI marketing guys came up with a stunt. They intended to release promotional singles under three additional different names: all anagrams of Roy Harper. There was Per Yarrow: a Norwegian classical avant-garde composer; Harry Rope: a leather-clad rocker; and Rory

Phare: a lounge lizard and trendy art designer. All were in addition to the one released under Roy's real name.

The idea was to release four singles under the four names, each with a different cover featuring Roy dressed appropriately (in disguise), and present the pseudonyms to the music critics without them knowing it was Roy. It was hoped that this method would avoid any prejudice.

But things went rather awry. To start with, EMI chose not to support the idea as promised. The singles were not widely distributed nor given much of a push. Those sent to critics were at first well-received. But as soon as the critics twigged it was Roy, the mood changed and the stunt backfired. The critics did not appreciate being played, and consequently, some of the reviews were harsh.

Once again, the album did not sell well. In 1994, it was re-released on Roy's Science Friction label, as *Garden Of Uranium*.

'Laughing Inside'
The production is a deliberate attempt to adopt a more modern style. The drum rhythm is prominent and steady, with guitars in the background, bubbling bass and keyboards underpinning the vocal. The main backing vocal is Nick Harper, and he plays great acoustic guitar towards the end.

'Laughing Inside' is a love song for Jacqui. It was selected as the single and is certainly better than Roy's usual single attempts, but it still failed to sell in any quantity.

'Garden Of Uranium'
I first heard this – one of the most powerful songs in the collection – on the main studio speakers and was completely blown away. It was a return to Roy and his guitar. The backing doesn't intrude too much. Nick's slide guitar accentuates the mood, with the bass and keyboards restrained, allowing the guitar to dominate. The song itself is straightforward, without too many poetic layers or obfuscations.

Roy had moved to Lincolnshire, only to discover plans afoot for a nuclear dump at Killingholme – fifteen miles from his house. He wasn't happy. The tenet of the song is that people are more important than profit. The planet should not be polluted with nuclear waste that will still be around in hundreds of thousands of years. Roy was way ahead of his time in advocating renewable energy from sun, wind and tide.

'Still Life'
An evocative musical poem describing a freezing winter scene. Roy is looking out the window at the cold landscape in the twilight of the late afternoon. Time has also frozen. A jackdaw sits on a telegraph pole. The sky shimmers with watery pastel pinks. The shadows reveal the perfect impression of a bird's wings as it tried to land in the snow. All nature is watching, and trying to survive in the extreme weather.

We hear the ticking of a clock, ethereal keyboards, the odd strumming guitar and rumbling bass. Roy's voice so plaintive.

The song has the feel of a painting: the winter scene captured forever in the words, music, and the mind. Beautiful. Delicate. Sensitive. Perfect.

'Pinches Of Salt'

Over an acoustic guitar, Roy croons a fairy tale to the 'tune of the moon on the ocean'. The backing builds – the bass, keyboards and percussion creating a dreamy atmosphere on which to paint the whimsical poem. And we are there in the fairy story: turning away from nature, as spray by spray, act by act, we destroy the planet, until, finally, the wolf beats down the door.

'Desert Island'

This is the track I thought should've been the single. It has a modern backing with what sounds like a xylophone but is probably Nick on a keyboard. The sea sounds and a really upbeat lyric give the track a bright immediacy. The embellishments and chirpy backing vocal (from Jacqui) all work well. The saxophone solo is superb and Roy's acoustic Ovation sounds perfect. The melody is also very engaging. I could see this getting into the charts.

The song was actually a small section from one of Roy's 20-minute epics: 'Burn The World' (which would surface later as a single). The lyric concept is great: the wish to retreat from the capitalist society nightmare and settle somewhere idyllic, even if only in the cocoon of your own room.

> I must say goodbye to the blindfold
> And pursue the ideal
> The planet becoming the hostess
> Instead of the meal
> Air, fire, water, earth, you were paradise
> I'm sorry about me

The dream to live in harmony with nature and not plunder it from greed ends with an apology to the planet on behalf of all mankind.

'Government Surplus'

A song about how young people – when deprived of work opportunities – are put through the sausage machine of society. They are disparagingly called lazy, and were once told to get on their bikes (a reference to politician Norman Tebbit's infamous slur). Men are surplus to requirements and made to queue for money, while young women produce assembly-line babies. The whole lie of society is propped up by the media propaganda. Roy is being overtly political and poetically direct. There is no complication or disguise in these lyrics.

The backing is Roy's acoustic guitar, with Nick providing fills, working around Roy with complex runs and machine-gun salvos of notes. They knit together so well.

'Surplus Liquorice'

This 38-second follow-on from 'Government Surplus' is a chilling track (not dissimilar to the Dead Kennedys' 'Kinky Sex Makes The World Go Round'), in which Margaret Thatcher talks about a revolutionary group intent on bringing down society.

'Liquorice Alltime'

A poem set to chaotic music, with a sung chorus of 'Place in our time': a play on 'Peace in our time'. The drums keep a steady, interesting rhythm, with staccato instrumentation of organ, guitar and fretless bass, all bursting in. Fun, but not an easy listen. It feels like the experiment it is.

The lyrics – like the music – come at you from all sides: a bombardment of words, meanings, puns, alliteration and nonsense, from which some sense can be gleaned. One gets the drift of society's insanity, with its sensationalism, drunken mindlessness, gunrunning and poverty. Roy stands in the middle, trying to make sense of it, looking for someone to take him home and help him forget.

'Maile Lei'

After the madness of the previous two songs, we come back to earth with a love song – just Roy and his guitar. Dedicated to his new wife, Jacqui, the song is a commemoration of their wedding, which took place on a beach in Hawaii. Maile is a dark green aromatic vine, and a lei is a garland of flowers. The Maile Lei is used on special occasions: in this instance, the marriage of Roy on Jacqui on May Day. The lyrics reflect Roy's hard times and how Jacqui had rescued him. Now she was his May Queen.

'Same Shoes'

This track is keyboard-and-drum-driven. The underlying throbbing fretless bass makes a noise reminiscent of whale sounds. Roy's voice is treated with a lot of echo, and there is variation in pace and instrumentation.

The song is about the recycling of fashions and images from previous decades in one endless stream of marketing. It's the 1950s all over again, with James Dean and Marilyn Monroe regurgitated for the next generation to consume.

Then there is the Cuban connection. Roy visited Cuba in the late 1960s. Wanting to have a conversation with a local, he had his shoes cleaned by an old man. Careful not to be overheard, he asked the man how things had been since the revolution. The man looked up at him and said, 'Same shoes': it stuck in Roy's mind, twenty years later surfacing in this song.

I almost made my debut as a rock star on this track. I visited Lincolnshire at the same time as Bob Owens. Roy was working on this album and wanted some unusual backing vocals. Bob, Jacqui and I were roped in to try something off-the-wall. Jacqui and Bob's attempts were deemed worthy of consideration, but mine were soon wiped, thus ending another potential turning point in my career. In the end, Roy did the backing vocals himself.

'Descendants Of Smith'

The title track is one of the album's stronger songs. There are no drums – it's mainly Roy on acoustic, with underlying fretless bass and keyboards. It has a futuristic musical feel, appropriate to the science fiction theme.

What incredible technology might our descendants possess in 4,000,000 years time? Smith – violently murdered – leaves his blood stain in the ice. 4,000,000 years later, his descendants have the ability to reconstitute him from his DNA, and even manipulate his genes to produce a mate for him. Smith finds himself in a zoo with other reconstituted exotic creatures. He is considered an unusual specimen, displayed as a living artefact from the past.

So who are these mysterious, advanced descendants of Smith? Are they still human beings?

'Laughing Inside' (Rough And Ready version)

The 'Rough And Ready' version is a sparse acoustic rendition, with Nick playing some exquisite runs to bass accompaniment. It's a showcase for Roy's singing and Nick's accomplished guitar-playing. Nothing is covered up. I prefer it to the more processed version because it is far less poppy – not my favourite song, though.

Single

'Laughing Inside' b/w 'Laughing Inside' (Rough and Ready version)

There were four cover varieties featuring different cover photos – of Roy Harper, Per Yarrow, Harry Rope and Roy Phare. Originally, the 'Rough And Ready' version was available on the single only but was included on the later CD release.

Loony On The Bus (1988)

First released by Awareness Records in 1988
Personnel:
Roy Harper: producer
Roy Harper: guitar, vocals and all songwriting
Dave Cochran: bass guitar
'Admiral' John Halsey: drums
Andy Roberts: guitars
Henry McCullough: electric guitar
Dave Lawson: keyboards
Preston Heyman: drums
Guy Mature
Tony Franklin: bass
John Leckie: engineer
Jacqui Harper: engineer
Recorded: Abbey Road, Folkingham/Lincolnshire
Artwork: Ben Harper/Jacqui Harper/Nick Harper

Roy and Jacqui were settled in their house at Folkingham. Their musical partnership had blossomed. Jacqui had proven to be an apt engineer and she soon became integral to both studio and live performance.

Following the last album's messy promotion and subsequent failure to break through, Roy and EMI parted ways for a second time. But on this occasion, he was in a far better financial state. Times were not so desperate – life was good. But without EMI, Roy still needed an income. So he organised a deal to release his albums through Awareness Records.

They needed a new release, but Roy and Jacqui had only recorded four new songs. So the decision was made to use the demos and partly-worked songs originally intended for *Commercial Breaks* back in 1977. For some reason – probably contractual – the title *Commercial Breaks* could not be used, and some tracks were not included. The resulting album – *Loony On The Bus* – was a mishmash, and it shows.

Roy was still smarting from the vitriolic criticism often aimed at him. A critic writing for Best (a women's magazine) described Roy as 'The loony you find yourself sitting next to on the bus'. He decided to own the comment, writing a song later to become the album title. Jacqui and Roy designed the album cover, using Nick's photo of Roy as the loony with Jacqui sitting beside him.

For some reason, 'My Little Girl' and 'Too Many Movies' – originally recorded for *Commercial Breaks* – were left off.

'No Change (Ten Years Ago)'
From *Commercial Breaks*.

'Sail Away'
From *Commercial Breaks*.

'I Wanna Be Part Of The News'
From *Commercial Breaks*.

'Burn The World (Part 1)'
This song is delivered in an eerie, semi-religious, high register, with acoustic guitar, underlying drone and echo, creating an ominous, chilling sound. Stark and novel, this lament is delivered in an anguished wail before crashing into a thundering guitar riff with welling undertones.

But this was a mere taster for the long epic Roy had waiting in the wings. He had already used one segment of it ('Desert Island') on *Descendants Of Smith*.

Our mad civilisation – in a religious frenzy, with lust for power or sheer greed – is about to engineer complete world destruction. The poem – with its 'I am the light, I am the way' – highlights religious texts and warns against the nuclear destruction we will probably unleash. 'Burning the world' will bring an end to life.

'Casualty'
This is the studio version. The live version was released in 1982 on the B-side of 'No One Gets Out Alive'. It's a stonking piece of fun, as Roy parodies his own career in a very 1980s production, delivered with hilarity. Dave Lawson's funky guitar and Tony Franklin's bubbling bass work well with the humourous lyric's zany delivery. The band really rocks and storms along, capturing the madness of the live performance.

They had great fun sampling the babies in the centre section too. Great stuff. It fits *Loony On The Bus* perfectly.

'Cora'
From *Commercial Breaks*.

'Playing Prison'
An acoustic number with strident guitar and heartfelt vocals. It's rather interesting to hear Roy whistling, which gives a whimsical feel. The chorus vocal harmonies are perfect and typical Roy. The end synthesizers create an orchestral feel that gives the track additional power.

'Playing Prison' is a song about breaking up. Roy remembers the heated words spoken when leaving Verna, here analysing his own thoughts and feelings. Does he regret leaving his children? He questions his motive for leaving. He is chasing perfection and refusing to fall into what he perceives as a trap; a convention; a role.

'Loony On The Bus'
The great opening electric riff immediately hits you, followed by the bass and thudding percussion. The riff persists, driving the song along at speed, giving energy.

Ostensibly, the brainless loony is making a loud noise, lighting his farts and behaving like a lout. He is the type that if you react to him in any way, your reaction will rebound on you. But if you listen to what this lout is actually mouthing off about, you find that it is climate change, the ozone layer and the destruction of lakes and forests by acid rain. And if all that isn't worth making a fuss about, then what is?

The lyric is a clever metaphor. The person sitting next to Roy on the bus is the critic who is writing him off, while Roy, the loony, articulates issues that desperately need addressing. Roy's songs are not just pop trivia. They have content and meaning. So who's the real loony?

'Come Up And See Me'
From *Commercial Breaks*.

'The Flycatcher'
From *Commercial Breaks*.

'Square Boxes'
From *Commercial Breaks*.

Once (1990)

First released on Awareness Records in 1990
Personnel:
Roy Harper: producer
Roy Harper: guitars, vocals and all songwriting (apart from verse one of 'Berliners')
Dave Gilmour: guitar
Nick Harper: guitar
Nigel Mazlyn Jones: guitar, dulcimer
Tony Franklin: bass
Steve Broughton: drums, percussion
Mark Feltham: harmonica
Jacqui Harper, Kate Bush, Terry Cooke: backing vocals
Jacqui Harper: engineer
John Carder Bush: photography
Ray Preacher: cover design

Profits from *Loony On The Bus* provided finance for this album's making. Again recorded at home, the sound was as crisp and sophisticated as any professional facility. The home studio was a warm, friendly atmosphere where people could relax, and work could proceed with no time restrictions.

Dave Gilmour played lead on three tracks, Nick Harper did some lead guitar, and the guitar wizard, Nigel Mazlyn Jones, appears on a couple of tracks. Kate Bush makes a guest appearance on the opening track. The main band members were the perennial Steve Broughton and Tony Franklin, with Mark Feltham on harmonica. Roy wanted a clean, guitar-based sound, similar to a live performance: a contrast to *Descendants Of Smith*. I think he achieved that.

This is an angry album – with Roy campaigning against cruelty to animals, war and division, society, climate change and fanatical religion – tempered by a couple of love songs. There may not be a 20-minute epic, but with the calibre of 'The Black Cloud Of Islam', 'Berliner', 'Once' and 'Ghost Dance' present, there is no shortage of quality content.

A concert at the Dominion Theatre on Tottenham Court Road on 22 November 1990 was filmed and released as *Roy Harper – Once – Live*. He did not rate the film, but he did like the album.

'Once'

'Once' is a powerful start, with Roy's guitar style distinctive. It begins with a statement that Earth is for all creatures, for all people, and for those without a voice. The vocal is delivered in a plaintive style. Life is for laughing, togetherness and love. As Roy barks the word 'once', the chorus crashes in with Dave Gilmour and Kate Bush. We are reminded that we only have one life; one chance at getting it right; one chance to treat everything with the respect we would have for ourselves; one chance to wonder at the universe and savour the moment. One chance is all we have. Joy, love and hope. Just once.

The chorus is highly potent. The changes in pace and intensity add to the tension, and Gilmour's note purity adds a dimension of genius. Kate's voice has her characteristic beautiful waver. On the last two choruses, the band gives its all, with power chords providing a heavier vibe.

'Once In The Middle Of Nowhere'

Not so much a song, as a strange discordant minute, with a synthesizer drone and a catalogue, read aloud in distorted voices. It makes for a disturbing interlude. Interest rapidly fades after the first few listens! It segues into the next track.

'Nowhere To Run To'

This could be the anthem for the Animal Liberation Front. Animals are often mistreated. They are used to attract tourists to zoos, test products in labs, and are slaughtered for our consumption – they have nowhere to run to. We humans are the cruel, uncaring monsters who will do anything for profit. Not many people write songs about it, though. But Roy did.

The treatment is simple: stark guitar, ominous bass and a wailing harmonica. The vocal is angry: in fact, I have rarely heard Roy so angry.

'The Black Cloud Of Islam'

The anger continues into this track. Roy says he thought long and hard about releasing this song because he didn't want to be accused of racism. The song is not about race. It is against claustrophobic religions that indoctrinate and are horrendously intolerant. Fundamentalist religion runs contrary to everything Roy believes in: freedom, rationality, tolerance, equality and togetherness.

This song was written in the aftermath of both the fatwa on Salman Rushdie following the publication of his novel, 'The Satanic Verses', and the terrible Lockerbie plane bombing. An explosive device was detonated on Pan Am Flight 103, causing it to crash on the Scottish town of Lockerbie, killing all 271 people onboard and eleven local residents. It was just one in a series of bombings. Roy wasn't infuriated only by the vengeful bloodlust; he also was reacting to oppression, rigid compliance, misogyny and politics. He did fear retribution, but this did not deter him, and he dared to release the song.

As with 'Nowhere To Run To', the production is quite basic: a strident acoustic guitar, snarling vocal and nothing else. There is the feel of a live recording. As with other angry songs like 'I Hate The White Man', he didn't want his anger to be diluted.

'If'

This song combines a soft finger-picking, a sweet melody and soaring vocals, with Tony Franklin's soft bass, Nick Harper's lead guitar, and Terry Cooke's backing vocals. It feels like a love song but is, in fact, a continuation of the previous song's theme: describing the same issues from a different angle. As was the case with 'South Africa' a soft approach is deployed instead of fury.

It is amusing to imagine Roy 'Having it out with God': he might apologise for not believing in the fairy tale. As he says in the song: 'Difference is beautiful and living it is bliss'.

'Winds of Change'
Another change of pace and tone to a steady drum rhythm and a punchy vocal. It's a repeating refrain for a minute and a half, with political commentary questioning the leaders of the day and asking where it's all leading. Are we going to be around in the future, or are we just a flash in the pan?

'Berliners'
This song was written to commemorate the 50th anniversary of the beginning of World War II. Roy thinks that the people who fought for freedom and a better world were betrayed. The vocal is passionate, flawless and as clear as spring water. Roy, Dave Gilmour and Tony Franklin merge together beautifully in the instrumental section towards the end. Only Gilmour can create those crystal clear note sustains that punctuate the song.

It starts with 'The Last Post' and words from the remembrance service in Spilsby, near where Roy was living. Verse one is the fourth stanza of the Laurence Binyon poem, 'Ode To Remembrance'. Roy's completes the song with words about the coming down of the Berlin Wall and the spirit that brings us together. This is followed by a diatribe against the pack of lies that the British Empire was built on. We are then reminded that we are the beneficiaries of the freedoms that previous generations died for. We enjoy the fruits of their sacrifice.

Underlying the song is the sound of the BBC reporting on the fall of the Berlin wall. This is a topic that Roy was and is extremely passionate about.

'Sleeping At The Wheel'
This is one of Roy's classic love songs and a contrast to the stronger material preceding it. It's a poem about waking beside the one you love in the early morning, listening to birdsong, and looking lovingly at her sleeping form – keeping watch over her, half-dreaming, and drifting off to sleep again.

It's an acoustic number where the band extend the scope and add to the mood. Roy excels at this type of love song. They are quite unique.

'For Longer Than It Takes'
The album's second acoustic love song is probably even better than 'Sleeping At The Wheel'. It was written for Jacqui at a time when their love was young and intense, and the vocal's tenderness conveys that deep emotion. Love songs are a Roy forte, and this one ranks as one of his best.

'Ghost Dance'
The final track begins with gentle acoustic guitar and an underlying bass drone, then changing as the rocking chorus cuts in. The two guitars really rock, and

by the protracted ending, they are in a heavy Native American rhythm. The balance is highly successful: the softer verses interspersed with the weightier choruses.

Roy is saying that we are living in a society that is squandering the future in exchange for just a handful of beads. We think we can change the world, but we're only dreaming. The world is changing. The climate is changing. New epochs arise. We shall be cast aside – a layer in the rock – as a new beginning starts without us. There's no way of stopping it.

Like the Native American Ghost Dances of the 19th century, we turn to superstition in the face of our own extinction. The Native Americans faced genocide at the hands of the white invaders. A Native American prophet – named Wodziwob – of the Palute tribe in Nevada, had a vision during a solar eclipse on 1 January 1869. The vision foretold of the return of their dead, the driving out of the white man, and return to a life of peace and plenty. The warriors were told to don the ghost shirts and dance in order to gain immunity from the white man's bullets. The superstition spread rapidly from tribe to tribe. They all desperately wanted to believe. It came to a sad end at the battle of Wounded Knee, where the ghost shirts proved useless, and the warriors were massacred. Roy here uses this as an analogy for the present time.

SOPHISTICATED BEGGAR

China girl is a sound goldfish is a childrens song sophisticated beggar is my rave my friend is in a distant land big fat silver aeroplane is for the junkies blackpool is where the rain falls like diamonds pin pricks the still water spreadeagles its laughter across the green sheet of the sleeping sea legend is for all of you girlie is a poem october the twelfth 1966 black clouds is a jazz tune mr. stationmaster is a pop song some people are forever committed is madness

Roy Harper

SIDE ONE:

China girl
Goldfish
Sophisticated beggar
My friend
Big fat silver aeroplane
Blackpool
Legend

SIDE TWO:

Girlie
October 12th
Black clouds
Mr. Stationmaster
Forever
Committed

STRIKE RECORDS
JHL 105
A PETER RICHARD PRODUCTION

COVER DESIGN LON GODDARD
PHOTO MIKE BERKOFSKY

Left: The back cover of *Sophisticated Beggar* – the first album released in 1966, which depicted Roy as a young beatnik. (*Science Friction*)

Below: A photo of Roy in 2019 that the author took from the wings at the Leeds Variety Hall concert. (*Opher Goodwin*)

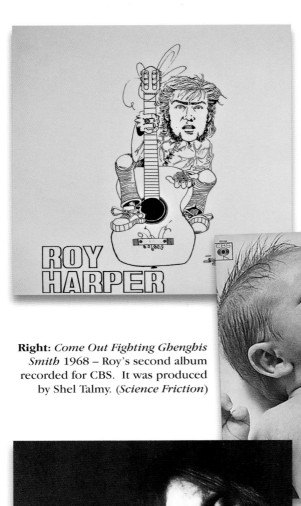

Left: The front cover of the author's highly valued *Sophisticated Beggar* album from 1966. (*Opher Goodwin*)

Right: *Come Out Fighting Ghenghis Smith* 1968 – Roy's second album recorded for CBS. It was produced by Shel Talmy. (*Science Friction*)

Left: *Folkjokeopus*, 1969. Roy plays the jester with pet monkey on his shoulder, although Roy wanted the cover to be diamond-shaped. The album is a showcase for the classic 'McGoohan's Blues'. (*Science Friction*)

Right: *Flat Baroque and Berserk*, 1970. The album marked the start of Roy's fruitful time with producer Pete Jenner on the EMI Harvest label. (*Science Friction*)

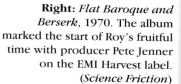

Left: Just four epic tracks, but *Stormcock* (1971), is widely seen as a masterpiece and Roy's best album. (*Harvest*)

Right: *Lifemask*, 1973. Not exactly a soundtrack for the film *Made*, more a vehicle for the incredible epic 'The Lord's Prayer'. (*Science Friction*)

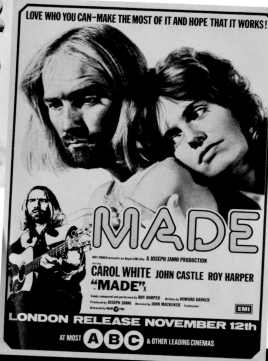

Right: Roy and Andy Roberts having a chat between songs at Knebworth in 1978. (*Paul Bednall*)

Below: The Roy Harper Band in full swing circa 1982, with Roy concentrating on the words. (*Keith Leslie*)

Right: Roy looking whimsical during a solo gig at the Poynton Folk Club in the 1980s. (*Pete Mellor*)

Left: *Valentine*, 1974. An album that extended the definition of a love song. (*Harvest*)

Right: *HQ* from 1975. The rockiest of Roy's albums features an array of superb musicians, including Dave Gilmour, Chris Spedding, Bill Bruford and Dave Cochran. (*Science Friction*)

Left: *Bullinamingvase*, 1978. Roy looks rather Machiavellian behind a feather. I think it's just one of those days in England … (*Science Friction*)

Right: *The Unknown Soldier*, 1980. It was after this album that Roy and Harvest parted company. (*Science Friction*)

Below: *Work of Heart*, 1982. The album was released on Roy's own label as he picked up the pieces after his divorce from EMI. (*Science Friction*)

Above: *Born in Captivity*, 1984. A limited-edition of acoustic demos for *Work of Heart* with a cover designed by James Edgar. (*Science Friction*)

Left: *Unhinged*, 1993. The CD release of the limited live cassette *Born in Captivity II*. (*Science Friction*)

Left: Roy is wearing the white silk scarf given to him by Jimmy Page and clutches his ovation guitar at the Caedman Hall, Gateshead in 1985. (*Keith Leslie*)

Right: Roy is sporting a pirate's eyepatch as a Descendant of Smith, circa 1988. (*Shaun D. Ibbott*)

Below: Outside the 12-Bar Club in 1997 with a motley crew. (*John Irvine*)

Right: Roy shares a moment with Jimmy Page and Dave Burnham. (*Simon Foster*)

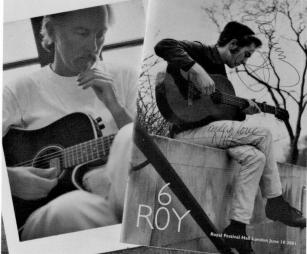

Left: The author's program from the Royal Festival Hall gig in 2001.

Right: Roy and the author at the Baltic for the screening of *The Magpie Index* in 2010. (*Liz Goodwin*)

Left: *Whatever Happened to Jugula*, 1985. The album co-starred Jimmy Page and paved the way for a return to EMI. (*Science Friction*)

Right: *Descendants of Smith*, 1988. The album was recorded for EMI at Roy's home studio in Lincolnshire. (*EMI*)

Left: *Loony On The Bus*, 1988. The album includes tracks from *Commercial Breaks*, which was never released by EMI, plus three new songs. It was made to finance the recording of *Once*. (*Awareness*)

Right: *Once*, 1990. An angry album recorded for Awareness Records, featuring Dave Gilmour and Kate Bush. (*Awareness*)

Left: *Burn The World*, 1990. Roy is shown in tribal mode with plaits, burning the world in two epic versions, one live and one in the studio. (*Science Friction*)

Right: *Death Or Glory*, 1992. The album was recorded in the aftermath of Roy's marriage break-up. (*Science Friction*)

Left: Roy caught mid-song! (*Andrew Bott*)

Right: Nick Harper looking towards his dad while the orchestra listens and waits at the Royal Festival Hall in 2011. (*Opher Goodwin*)

Left: Roy, sporting a cavalier beard, looks relaxed and cheerful before the show at the Royal Festival Hall in 2016. (*Opher Goodwin*)

Right: Roy acknowledges his friend and accompanist Bill Shanley at the Leeds Variety Hall in 2019. (*Opher Goodwin*)

Below: The whole ensemble in action at the Leeds Variety Hall in 2019. (*Opher Goodwin*)

Right: A study in concentration as Roy focusses on the music at the Leeds Variety Hall in 2019. (*Opher Goodwin*)

Left: *Commercial Breaks* 1994
The full, unreleased album
of demos recorded for EMI,
although many tracks had
already been released on *Loony
On The Bus*. (*Science Friction*)

Right: 1997's *Poems, Speeches,
Thoughts and Doodles* is an
album of spoken word pieces.
(*Science Friction*)

Left: *The Dream Society*,
1998. The cover features
stick men cave paintings
on an album awash with
nostalgia. (*Science Friction*)

Right: *The Green Man*, 2000. The cover has Roy peering through the green foliage in a largely acoustic return to his roots. (*Science Friction*)

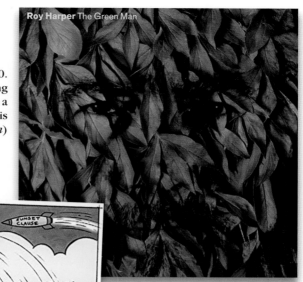

Roy Harper The Green Man

Roy Harper The Death Of God

I WILL INTERVENE

SUNSET CLAUSE

HISTORY WILL PROVE ME RIGHT

FREEDOM OF INFORMATION

HUMAN RIGHTS

PREVENTION OF TERRORISM ACT

HISTORY

Left: *The Death of God*, 2005. A cartoon cover with Tony Blair taking a dive through the WMD of history while God fails to intervene. (*Science Friction*)

Right: *Man and Myth*, 2013. Roy becomes the mythical beast as he takes us through a remarkable odyssey. (*Bella Union*)

ROY HARPER
MAN & MYTH

Left: An array of *Hors D'Oeuvres* – the Harper fanzine. I'm just missing vol. 4. Any offers?

Below: The flyer for *The Magpie Index,* a film by Richard Grayson featuring a number of monologues by Roy.

The Magpie Index

A new commission by Locus+ and the De La Warr Pavilion

A portrait of the legendary singer-songwriter Roy Harper by Richard Grayson

Below: A ticket for Roy's concert at the Dublin National Stadium in 1977.

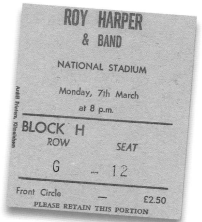

ROY HARPER
& BAND

NATIONAL STADIUM

Monday, 7th March
at 8 p.m.

BLOCK H
ROW
G — 12
SEAT

Front Circle — £2.50

PLEASE RETAIN THIS PORTION

Ardill Printers, Kilmainham

BLOOMSBURY THEATRE
GORDON STREET WC1
Tube. Euston. Euston Square
8.00 P.M.   277
SAT 9 APRIL 1988
ROY HARPER
PLUS SPECIAL GUEST
JAMES VARDA
£6.00   DOOR 7

GALLERY   22
SLIPS
To be retained   P.T.O

Above: A ticket for the 1988 Bloomsbury Theatre gig for the princely sum of £6! Roy was supported by James Varda.

Burn The World (1990)

First released by Awareness Records in 1990
Personnel:
Roy Harper: producer
Roy Harper: acoustic guitar, vocals and songwriting
Dave Gilmour: guitar
Tony Franklin: bass
Kevin McAlea: keyboards
Steve Broughton: percussion
Engineer: Jacqui Harper
Photography: Colin Curwood

Roy wrote the song, 'Burn The World', in 1984. When re-signed to EMI, he'd presented them with the 20-minute demo, which they rejected on the basis of it not being a good commercial proposition.

But the song is amazing – its global warming concept even more relevant today. Roy sat on the recording for six years, intending to work further on the production – as he had successfully done with other epics like 'The Lord's Prayer' and 'Me And My Woman' – but it never came about. Without a major label contract, he lacked the finances to devote to such a project, and he knew things were unlikely to change any time soon. Yet he believed the song was important, and began including it in his live sets. He continued developing the piece, receiving positive audience responses. Rather than abandon the song altogether, he decided to put the demo out as it was. When I first heard he was to release the two 20-minute tracks (studio version and live version), I immediately said, 'That's a single then, Roy!'. And so it was.

The live version demonstrates the earlier-mentioned pedal effect technology, and Jacqui's mixing ability, using the effects to the maximum. At times it sounds like a full band. Once again, Roy lives up to the epithet of a one-man rock and roll band.

The song itself is in eight distinct sections:

I. 'Burn The World'
II. 'Change It'
III. 'The Last Laugh'
IV. 'My Home Is On The Water'
V. 'Live In Peace'
VI. 'Walkabout'
VII. 'Desert Island'
VIII. 'Burn The World (reprise)'

Some critics saw 'Burn The World' as experimental, with rather morbid disorientating atonal sounds. The shorter 'Burn The World – Part 1' had already been released – on 1988's *Loony On The Bus* – was written at about the same time and used the same theme.

The seventh section – 'Desert Island' – was later worked up as the amazing stand-alone song on the *Descendants Of Smith* album. This showed what could've been achieved had Roy the opportunity to develop the whole song as he wanted.

'Burn The World' (Studio)

Synthesiser starts the piece with the characteristic heavy guitar. Bongos, fretless bass and an intense vocal then follow, as the riff drives everything along. The question is asked: 'Why don't you burn the world?'.

Section two has a different rhythm, with xylophone and a harsh vocal, barking 'Change it, rearrange it, derange it'.

Section three moves back to acoustic guitar and a weird, anguished voice.

Section four starts with the sound of waves. It begins slowly, almost spoken as poetry, with some discordance and bluntness of speech.

Section five is more melodic with a soft backing of bubbling synthesizer.

Section six starts with a bass throb and picked guitar before the heavier guitar and sparkly synthesizer lift the tone into the song's most easy-listening section. Then Dave Gilmour's great electric solo breaks in before it's back to that chorus. 'The planet becoming the hostess instead of the meal' sticks out to me – such a great line.

Following a short middle-eight, the opening section returns before fading out with a sweet classical quartet, in almost a fairground sound. We fiddle while the world burns.

Roy has never shied away from tackling the issues that most avoid: religion, politics, death and Earth destruction. He is fearless, passionate and determined. Some of the poetry here seems rather simple and perhaps not up to Roy's usual standard, but the sentiment is sincere and fervent. He speaks of our arrogance and the way we enjoy hurting and exerting our power. We blindly trample and destroy the very planet that gives us life. Mindlessly, we poison and pour huge amounts of fossil fumes into the environment. Roy is with the activists: fighting against the politicians' greed, trying to protect the planet, although he knows that ultimately we can't win. He dreams of somewhere to escape to because all we can do is live our lives in harmony with nature and not plunder the world for profit.

Then follows a heartfelt apology for the mess we have made on behalf of himself and all mankind.

Roy suggests that we should listen to the quieter voices, the poets who care, whose words are in the wind asking why.

'Burn The World' (Live)

Recorded in 1989, live at the Bloomsbury Theatre, London.

Over the intervening years, Roy had worked on the song. You can hear the more complicated arrangement in the finger-picking: it is more mature than that of the studio demo. The performance is staggering, the emotional content astounding. Is there any need for a band when Roy can produce sounds like this?

Death Or Glory? (1992)

First released on Awareness Records in 1992
Personnel:
Roy Harper: producer, engineer
Roy Harper: guitar, vocals and all songwriting
Nick Harper: guitar
Tony Franklin: bass, keyboards
Steve Barnard: drums
Kate Bush: vocals
Michael Anthony: keyboards
Gerry Fehiley: drums
Colm O'Sullivan: keyboards
Cara Mastrey: backing vocals
Ray Barron: bouzouki
Roger Christopher: engineer
Recorded at Roy's studio in Clonakilty
Marcel Tromp: cover photo
Lippa Pearce: design

This recording was made at a difficult time. Roy and Jacqui had moved to
Ireland, taken on a huge old house, and were in the process of setting up
a studio. Work had begun on the album before everything suddenly came
to an abrupt halt. Roy had been collaborating with violinist Nigel Kennedy.
Then, in a flood of publicity, Jacqui left Roy for Nigel. This was devastating,
leaving Roy bereft, with suicidal thoughts – not to mention the professional/
musical impact. Jacqui had become an integral part of Roy's work. There
was a 24-track tape machine in pieces, a series of demos, and a broken
Harper.

Roy went into a period of secluded introspection, blame and emotional
turmoil. Roger Christopher – a young student engineer – helped Roy
reassemble the equipment and get the studio up and running. But it was
hardly the most conducive circumstances for an album's recording. Roy had to
feel his way around the new equipment and learn about engineering, which
had been Jacqui's forte.

Over the ensuing months, he somehow managed to do it – not only pulling
himself together but channelling his emotion into some outstanding tracks.
Like a phoenix rising from the ashes, came the album *Death Or Glory?*.

Listening again now, two points jump out at me: Roy's then terrible fragile
state and his state of denial. Both are evident in the poems, 'The Plough' and 'If
I Can'. He really thought that he and Jacqui's separation would be temporary
and that by appealing to her, he could win her back. Indeed, the two poems
baring his soul – coupled with the cover (a photo of the two of them naked
on the beach in Hawaii where they were married) – were grand and desperate
gestures, made in hope.

A reconciliation was not to be. But the turmoil produced a great album of angry songs: about the environment, war, homelessness and the state of society; an album about an anguished break-up. It is full of passion, anger, regret, self-analysis, despair, love – and despite everything, hope.

In 1994, *Death Or Glory?* was re-released on Roy's Science Friction label, without the two poems ('If I Can' and 'The Plough'), which were replaced by a B-side: 'The Methane Zone'. The cover design, too, was different, bearing a grinning skull and crossbones with dripping blood-red captions. The album was again re-released – and also remastered – in 1998, this time with a cover photo of a rosebud infested with greenfly. This edition shared the 1994 track listing, but with two tracks partly re-recorded: 'The Fourth World' and 'Death Or Glory?'.

It's a difficult and shocking album to listen to. In addition to the beautiful poetry and music there to dwell on and absorb, there is deep sadness and anguish that most of us can relate to.

It was a good decision to leave 'Man Kind', 'The Plough' and 'If I Can' off subsequent reissues. The poems are too extreme and personal for repeated listening.

'Death Or Glory?'
Roy certainly got his stick back on the ice – as Canadian band, The Tea Party (with whom he toured in Canada) would say. It is full-tilt into the fray; the music charges into battle with great intent. The story of 'the split' is told in rousing terms. The track rampages forward in a last-ditch effort, flinging all caution to the wind. A rousing drum rhythm gallops along, with fast pulsing bass and Nick's electric guitar swirling through it.

While the lyrics recount the separation – 'No warning, no mercy/Off with his head/Not even one last kiss' – they also recall the good times: 'We lived in heaven, hearts and minds'. For all its ferocity, the song is Roy's desperate plea for the two to reconcile: 'We can make it there again? Our strength will be then/ Baby, down to you/Baby, up to me'. It's a full-on album introduction.

'The War Came Home Tonight'
In 1991, in the run-up to this album, the Gulf War was happening. We watched the TV as cruise missiles blew buildings to pieces and hundreds of people were killed before our eyes, although we never saw any blood. Because of this divorce from reality, the Gulf War was more like a computer game than an actual war. Roy wrote this song while watching the action play out on the box, to a backdrop of jingoistic fervour.

Starting off in military-style, chanting 'left, right, left, right' – later changing to 'wrong, right, wrong, right' – Roy sounds like he is marching into war. The marching drum and guitar persist, as he describes the sensationalism of war: every TV network seeks to win in the ratings battle, and the viewers consume without considering the rights or wrongs of what they are watching. The media treat the event as 'A crisis to manipulate' for their own ratings. Roy modified that old toothpaste advertisement, 'You'll wonder where the yellow went, when you brush your teeth with Pepsodent', to 'You'll wonder where the country went in the target-rich environment'.

This is an anti-war song with a difference. War is sanitised for mass viewing in our living rooms. We watch it as entertainment from a distance. The track finishes appropriately, with a marching drum.

'Duty'
Roy recites this poem as a military drum rhythm persists through the first verse. A bell chimes: the bell of doom; the death knell. An ominous chant wells up behind the words. The bell chimes again as the poem proceeds. Is it our duty as human beings to protect the planet? Or is it the will of 'God' to allow chemical processes to produce a greenhouse hell in which most of life, including us, will struggle to survive? 'So sayeth the Lord'.

The short, simply-arranged track hits home for me. The lyrics are pertinent and thought-provoking. It's one I keep coming back to.

'Waiting For Godot Part Zed'
A poignant, melancholy song, delivered with a delicate guitar, fretless bass, and a touch of bubbling synthesizer. The bass echoes the sad refrain for this intensely beautiful tale of a broken heart at the sudden ending of a love affair. Roy is remembering and reliving love's embraces. Through his tears, he is left waiting for Godot, empty and bereft. Sadly, we all know that Godot never appears.

'Next To Me'
Another dose of anguish and regret. Roy's voice appears to be on the verge of breaking as he delivers words packed with emotion. Memories and regrets emerge as he relates the tragic sorrow of parting and the heartbreak of lying awake alone. Listening to the house's unsettling creaking, Roy wishes his mind to be free of her while longing for her to return and share his bed again. It segues into the poem.

'Man Kind'
A short poem of graphic detail, 'Man Kind' describes a nightmare in which Roy is spread-eagled and executed by Jacqui as she rips his aorta. He asks that she also cut his windpipe, so he can spray the blood into her face with his last breath. This poem of torment was deemed too raw for subsequent re-releases: the anguish was too personal.

The song signals a change of direction: away from the deeply introspective dissection of the break-up's devastating effect into a fantasy nightmare.

'The Tallest Tree'
The guitar picking here has a South American flavour. The chorus is catchy and memorable.

Roy directs his fury at the western consumption and profit-making that presently ravages the world. The primary focus is the destruction of the Brazilian rainforest and the man who stood tall to oppose it. Chico Mendes was a rubber tapper, an environmentalist and trade unionist. He organised opposition to the forest destruction whilst looking for sustainable ways of living in harmony with it. The ranchers who wanted to clear the forest for grazing cattle, murdered him. It's a tribute to a man who – despite knowing the danger – was prepared to stand and fight.

'The Tallest Tree' is a song of hope: if we all stand together, we can find a better way of living. We do not have to follow a path of destruction. We can change the world for the better.

'Miles Remains'

Largely instrumental, this extremely unusual and dreamy piece of music has lots of echo. The guitars play unusual chords and chiming notes in slow configurations, with underlying bass and synth. The vocal has a calming, almost meditative effect, unlike any of Roy's previous work.

Roy has always been a jazz fan. Miles Davis died in 1991, and this song is a tribute to the inventor of cool. Miles may be gone, but his music remains.

'The Fourth World'

There is nothing meditative about this track. It storms along from the start. There is a churning rhythm as Roy piles on the groove with a heavy guitar riff. The music gallops along for seven minutes: not a second too long.

This was not going to be a hit single or receive any airplay. The expletive-ridden middle eight may be a tad over the top but certainly stirs the blood. Fortunately, Roy was no longer with EMI, and he could do what he wanted without having to justify or pander to any commercial interest. Consequently, without filters or restraint, he pours forth all his pent-up fury in a vitriolic attack on our violent, destructive society. But of the tirade against our leaders and their philosophy, there appears hope. We have two chances: we can go on as we are and destroy the world or build something sustainable. We can gather around fires and come together: 'One global village with faces as bright as the sun'.

'Why?'

What can possibly follow a stonking seven-minute number like 'The Fourth World'? The answer is a 40-second poem, sung a cappella, a short guitar run and some strums. 'Why do you have to gain so much to lose the world?'

'Evening Star'

Now there's a total tone change to a love song delivered with extraordinary acoustic guitar work. Fretless bass adds a drone, and Cara Mastery offers delicious backing vocals on the last choruses.

This was written for Robert Plant's daughter, Carmen, and was performed live at her wedding to Charlie Jones (bass player with Plant's band). It is a delightful song. Do I detect a nod to 'Stairway To Heaven' in the lyrics?: ('There's a lady who knows…')

The track's position in the sequence feels a little incongruous, sandwiched between the strident 'The Fourth World' and 'Cardboard City'.

'Cardboard City'
This starts with Roy's chugging guitar against Nick Harper's bluesy second guitar. Nick's playing progresses into some smashing slide. The pair's individual playing styles interact powerfully.

This is Roy's response to the world's growing number of homeless people.

'One More Tomorrow'
A wonderfully aching cry for lost love. Roy bares his soul in another plea for her to return. His voice is plaintive and emotionally pure. The juxtaposition of angelic voice and harsh guitar creates tension, the guitar belying the melody's delicacy. It is violent and displays inner anguish. The reminiscences are painful, the confessions sincere.

'The Plough'
A heart-wrenching self-analytical poem, painting a picture of a befuddled Roy, lost in grief. He sits alone at the top of the stairs, full of remorse and regret.

'On Summer Day'
A wistful love song performed solo. It's a moving story of love won and lost; a song of longing, and holding perfection in the hand, only to watch it fly away. The high falsetto lilts and radiates sadness. It's a song for anyone who has suffered loss. Will she ever come back?

'If I Can'
The album ends with the tearful lines: 'If I could, I would/If I can, I will'. The rest of the poem is printed on the sleeve but does not appear on the CD.

Single
'Death Or Glory?'/'The War Came Home Tonight' b/w 'Duty'/'The Methane Zone'.
This four-song single comprises three of the album tracks and a demo: 'The Methane Zone'. On that song, Roy interpolates a couple of old blues/gospel classics: 'Bury My Body' (also known as 'Lord I Don't Care Where They Bury My Body' or 'My Soul Is Gonna Live With God') – an old gospel song (covered by the Animals on their first album); and an Elmore James (and others) blues classic: 'Early One Morning'. I doubt there are many songs about flatulation. I am only aware of one other: Screaming Jay Hawkins'

7

'Constipation Blues'. It's just a bit of fun. Roy was never one to shy away from the lavatorial.

'The Methane Zone' was included on later *Death Or Glory?* reissues.

Born In Captivity II (1992)/Unhinged (1993)

Limited edition tape released by the Hard Up2 Label 1992
CD released on the Science Friction label in 1993
Personnel:
Roy Harper: producer, vocal, acoustic guitar, all songwriting
Nick Harper: acoustic guitar
Graeme Fowler: drums
Jacqui Harper: engineer

This live album marks a watershed. The recordings come from 1989/1991, prior to Roy and Jacqui's split and were first released as a tape called *Born In Captivity II.*

It is tremendous. My favourite track is 'Short And Sweet' – such a powerful version. Unfortunately, that track was omitted when the CD was released in 1993 as 'Unhinged'.

Born In Captivity II contains three songs/poems that don't appear anywhere else: 'Back To The Stones', 'Three Hundred Words' and 'Yet'. Thankfully, two of these are on the CD version.

It's a superb collection showcasing Roy and Nick working so well together. Nick features on 'Descendants Of Smith', 'When An Old Cricketer Leaves The Crease', 'Hope', 'Highway Blues' and 'Same Old Rock'.

'Three Hundred Words' was written for Graeme 'Foxy' Fowler: the well-known English cricketer. Foxy joins Roy and Nick, on drums, for a rendition of 'Hope'.

I live in the hope that full recordings of these concerts exist and will one day spawn a *Born In Captivity 3,* 4, 5 and 6'. Wouldn't that be something?

Side One
'Descendants Of Smith' – Wulfrun Hall, Wolverhampton 1991
'Short And Sweet' – Wulfrun Hall, Wolverhampton 1991
'When An Old Cricketer Leaves The Crease' – Wulfrun Hall, Wolverhampton 1991
'Three Hundred Words'/'Hope' – Withenshawe, Manchester 1991
'Naked Flame' – Bloomsbury Theatre 1990
'South Africa' – Bloomsbury Theatre 1990
'North Country' (Trad.) – Wulfrun Hall, Wolverhampton 1991

Side Two
'Commune' – Bloomsbury Theatre 1990
'Yet' (A Poem) – Civic Theatre, Leeds 1989
'Back To The Stones' – Queens Hall, Edinburgh 1989
'Legend' – Bloomsbury Theatre 1990
'Frozen Moment' – Civic Theatre, Leeds 1990
'Highway Blues' – Wulfrun Hall, Wolverhampton 1991
'The Same Old Rock' – Withenshawe, Manchester 1991

'Three Hundred Words'

A poem for cricketer Graham 'Foxy' Fowler that acts as a reminiscence. Roy and girlfriend Pat Tetly were watching Foxy Fowler batting for England in a West Indies versus England cricket match.

'Yet' (A Poem)

It is nostalgic to hear the old repartee between Roy and his audience. He is relaxed, the audience warm and full of banter, taking me straight back to those days. But there is rapt attention as he reads the poem.

The poem is a polemic on society: the mindless emptiness of the tabloids, propaganda thugs and purposeless clones.

'Back To The Stones'

The distinctive acoustic guitar sets interesting patterns as Roy recounts the tale of a Stonehenge festival and the 'Battle Of The Bean Field'.

The travelling community – and many alternative groups – used to gather every year on 21 June for a festival at Stonehenge in Wiltshire. The locals protested against this gathering, and the police – with government backing – waged war on the travellers. The festival was banned. The police attacked people, terrorised their children and wrecked vehicles and homes. A distraught pregnant woman was dragged away by her hair. The song is a celebration of the Stonehenge festival and a condemnation of the Police' prejudice and brute force.

Poems, Speeches, Thoughts And Doodles (1997)

Personnel:
Roy Harper: producer
Roy Harper: spoken word, guitar and all poems
Jeff Martin: guitar
Darren Crisp: mastering
Colin Curwood: photography

This album is predominantly poetry. It started life as a mail-order CD, later made more widely available. The poems are read without musical accompaniment, though there are occasional bursts of guitar. Some of the poems appeared as songs on previous albums, and one appears later.

Jeff Martin (From Canadian band The Tea Party) was staying with Roy at the time and contributed to the album. He is credited with co-writing 'Timelords In The Frost': the album's introduction piece.

It starts with a minute of Roy doodling on guitar. He recites the poems in his rich, expressive voice, mostly straight, with occasional studio chicanery as was heard on 'The Lord's Prayer' from *Lifemask*. The production certainly adds interest.

It is fascinating to hear Roy emphasise and accentuate phrasing in the poems that were previously songs. He expresses different personal emotions in poems such as 'Our Father' that never appear in song. They reveal Roy's other layers.

There is one song on the album: 'Love Me' – a simple, solo acoustic number. It's a paean to love, to his woman, or perhaps the planet.

1. **'First Thing In The Morning'** (*Unknown Soldier*)
2. **'Blow By Blow'**
3. **'The Spirit Lives'** (*HQ*)
4. **'Lunchtime Sandwich Secretaries'**
5. **'November'**
6. **'The Arty Fartique (The Critic)'**
7. **'Bad Speech 2'** (An enlargement of 'Bad Speech' from *Whatever Happened To Jugula?*)
8. **'Timelords In The Frost'** (Harper/Martin)
9. **'Angel Of The Night'** (*Dream Society*)
10. **'Hidden By Numbers'**
11. **'Hole In The Sky'**
12. **'Overnight Success'**
13. **'Nero'**
14. **'Clones'**
15. **'Constant Sorrow'**(A cappella)
16. **'BUPA'**
17. **'Extreme Middle Age'**
Guitar interlude

18. 'The Night Aglow'
19. 'Filthy Stain Hussein'
20. 'Your Tongue In Their Cheeks' (Sung with tongue in cheek and faint backing)
21. 'Commune' (*Valentine*)
22. 'Tel'
23. 'Descendants Of Smith' (*Descendants Of Smith*)
24. 'Our Father'
25. 'Crystal Shoes '
26. 'The Afternoon Sun'
27. 'The Unknown'
28. 'And Yet' (Fading into a burst of angry guitar)
29. 'Auto Farrier'
30. 'Ere Winter Ends'
31. 'Ghost Dance' (*Once*)
32. 'Pinches Of Salt' (*Descendants Of Smith*)
33. 'The Song That Never Ends'
34. 'Love Me (a song)'

The Dream Society (1998)

Science Friction label
Personnel:
Roy Harper: producer
Roy Harper: acoustic guitar, vocals, tambourine, washboard and all songwriting
Ian Anderson: flute
Steve Barnard: drums, percussion
Nick Harper: acoustic guitar, slide guitar, electric guitar
Noel Barrett: bass
John Fitzgerald: keyboard, piano, trumpet, concertina, harp
Felix Howard: bass
Misumi Kosaka: vocals
Colm O'Sullivan: keyboards
Ric Sanders: violin
Bonnie Shaljean: harp
Jeff Ward: slide guitar, bass, hand drum, mandolin, percussion
John Leckie: engineer
Jeff Ward: engineer
Recorded in Roy's home studio in Clonakilty
George Fort: Cover art and drawings
Harry Pearce: Idea for front cover

An intensely personal album, full of various biographical details from Roy's life. It's a more introspective album than usual. Now in his 50s, he reflects on many influential lifetime events: his mother's death, his stepmother and her religion, brushes with the law, prison and mental institutions, pregnant girlfriends, relationships, fatherhood, busking and a showbiz career. He's been a lifelong rebel, putting himself outside of a society whose ethos he despises. Time to take stock?

The album was first to be titled The Seven Ages Of Man, and then Love Songs. Roy went to India on a writing retreat. During that period of self-imposed isolation, the album metamorphosed a number of times.

Visiting Roy in Ireland, I was fortunate to hear the early demos, which featured some amazing slide guitar. They were quite raw and different to the more refined later versions. At the time, I told him he ought to keep the raw demos to release in the future, as they had a different vibe to the completed album. Unfortunately, Roy didn't release them, which is a shame, as I would've liked to hear them again.

The original album came out in a limited edition, with a bonus disc featuring song extracts with Roy's spoken commentary, which gave captivating insight to the songs.

'Songs Of Love'

There is Spanish-sounding guitar to start the track as Misumi Kosaka sings. It's a tale in operatic style, about the first man and woman: a beginning of our culture's stories of love. I had not heard Roy sing like this before. But is it just about people or something wider? Perhaps it's the coming together of male and female, in the creation of all types of life?

'Songs Of Love Part 2'
This rushes in and motors along like a hectic love affair. It's a heavy sound that many a metal band would be proud of: a love song with a difference. The duet continues apace. Through the act of creation, universal awareness is achieved. We have life.

'Dancing All The Night'
There are hints of skiffle at the start, and some great slide guitar adds a heavier feel. It harks back to the 1940s and the wartime bombing of Manchester (Roy's first memory is being held in someone's arms, looking towards a glowing horizon, and hearing, 'Manchester is getting it tonight'): a time of spitfires and bluebirds.

The pace changes to quietly-picked guitar and the tragic tale of Roy's mother, who died shortly after his birth. She gave him life and left. Roy told me how he would peer into the mirror, searching for some resemblance. He describes a fantasy of dancing with his mother and seeing himself mirrored her features.

The music reflects the feel of 1940s/1950s dance songs.

'Psychopath'
The is loosely based on a 1950s skiffle song called 'Streamline Train', with added slide guitar. Following battles at home (with his stepmother) and at school (he did not like the career path mapped out for him), Roy headed off on the road to busk his way around the world. He had to escape: 'To leave the psychopath behind' and escape from himself. He had other worlds and loves to find. The adventure is beginning.

'I Want To Be In Love'
The journey continues with one of Roy's intense love songs, played primarily with a guitar, adding strings and flute. The bass adds an underlying throb. Roy's intense wish is to be in love, constantly in love. It has driven him, appearing in song after song. This is a dream from Roy's youth that has persisted throughout his life. Native American rhythm and chanting closes the song.

'Drugs For Everybody'
This song chugs along with a steady rocking rhythm with a searing guitar solo.

'On board the gondolas with the broken rock 'n' rollers/Smoking shit and talking it'. Roy is painting a nightmare with a heavy dose of humour. It is a world that he, as a young man, was very familiar with.

This is the prospect of society, with legalised, government-sponsored drugs and everyone stoned out of their heads: 'No need for reality'. A future world in which science has extended life length to hundreds of years by treating every symptom with drugs, creating genetically modified people grafted on to baboons, living in a stupor, with the universe on hold.

Maybe that's what happens when drugs get into the wrong hands. It's a tongue-in-cheek, satirical anti-drugs song.

'Come The Revolution'
We're still following Roy's recurring life themes: love, drugs and social change. He is saying that the revolution was a 1960s dream without any basis. The establishment was never going to be pushed aside, and the rebels were all living in dreamland, including himself. Nevertheless, is he still dreaming he could change the world? Perhaps with the coming revolution? The state is in control. Big Brother is watching every little thing you do. Your life is observed in the most minute detail. Nothing changes. Come the revolution. Roll on the revolution.

'Angel Of The Night'
The hard rock presentation in a guitar-based marching rhythm reflects the lyric's harshness. The track powers along, the vocal rising in anguish. It is relentless. The guitar solo towards the end is aggressive and violent.

The lyrics are about the time of Roy and Jacqui's break-up: a period when he was left alone at home in Ireland, listening to the house creak as the wind blew in the middle of the night. He is beset by demons of his own imagination, bereft and contemplating death. This song is torn from the very depths of his depression. Describing the pain and despair of the relationship's end, he sings of his fears and doubts in a self-analysis.

'The Dream Society'
A change in both pace and emotion. A serene vocal over picked guitar develops into a chorus with a slow pounding rhythm that retains a mellow atmosphere. The pace picks up, progressing through the eight-minutes-plus with some soaring guitar and vocals, never losing that gentle groove.

After the nightmares, we find ourselves in the more placid waters of dreams. Roy has often lain half-awake in REM sleep, his mind envisioning his ideals. His dreams are expansive, as the song describes. They encompass the whole gamut of human experience, past and present. Love, hunting, fight and flight, memories and wishes, fun and games, fears and terrors: all wrapped up in the arms of Orpheus. Roy related to the underworld adventures of the Greek poet, musician and prophet. When Orpheus' great love – Eurydice – died, he journeyed to the underworld to bring her back to life. Roy could identify with that. Lost love has been a feature of his life. He could have chosen Morpheus (Greek God of sleep and dreams), but he decided on Orpheus. Out of Roy's dreams comes the music.

'Broken Wing'
An exceedingly intricate guitar-picking underpins this seven-minute track. The vocal is pure and expressive, sweeping up and around in sadness, and

is another example of a vocal style that Roy was unlikely to have used at the beginning of his career.

The violin interlude adds to the melancholy, and there is a hint of Vaughan Williams' 'The Lark Ascending', as Roy looks forward to better days and the mending of his broken wing. An eagle metaphor – soaring on the thermals and crashing to the ground– describes the wound of Roy's wrecked marriage. It's a sad lament with an element of optimism. Love: the worst pain and most profound pleasure.

'These Fifty Years'

Roy's voice is in fine form as he tackles this fifteen-minute epic, which is based on another dream. Jethro Tull's Ian Anderson accompanies the band on flute. The final verse adds harp and strings, which trail off into guitar and flute, with Roy giving some non-lexical vocables (as in 'la la la').

The idea of him strolling along in bizarre conversation with God and Tom Huxleym is quite amusing; God telling him he's been a bad boy with wine, women and drugs (no mention of song) is rather accurate.

Roy's opposition to religion goes back to childhood. I find the following section amusing. In a dream, God has a go at Tom Huxley (Darwin's mouthpiece/bulldog) for using fossil evidence in his arguments, Huxley then accusing God of setting in motion western society's capitalist system, with its mountains of possessions, and rape of the earth. There's a lot packed in here; the path to everlasting life; the stifling of humans by fundamentalist doctrine; the lack of understanding that we are just animals aboard this planet; the blindness of belief without proof, and the way blind faith shuts out the wonder of the universe.

Finally, there is a toast to the awe of an ever-changing universe. As dawn approaches and a new day in this reality offers further opportunities, Roy awakens from the dream.

Conclusion

So the album ends. It is not the seven ages of man, though it does involve many episodes from Roy's life. It really isn't songs of love either, although there is plenty of love in it. As for calling it *The Dream Society*, I can see how that describes the title track and the last song 'These Fifty Years', and perhaps even the way our society is based on a fabricated religious dream, but I'm not convinced it is the right title for the album. With it being made in the turmoil of the break-up aftermath, perhaps the title should have been Introspections?

Bonus CD

The first thousand CDs came with an additional full-length bonus CD containing an alternative version of the song 'The Dream Society', in a more basic style than the polished album version. The rest of the CD featured Roy talking about the tracks, along with song snippets. Although it's fascinating and insightful to hear Roy's thoughts, once you've heard it, you are unlikely to play the CD again.

The Green Man (2000)

Science Friction label
Personnel:
Roy Harper: producer
Jeff Martin: producer
Roy Harper: guitar, vocals and all songwriting
Jeff Martin: hurdy-gurdy, 12-string slide electric guitar, mandolin, recorder, bongos, tambourine, guitar, 6-string slide guitar.
John Fitzgerald: keyboard
Paddy Keenan: uilleann pipes, low D whistle
Colm O'Sullivan: mandolin, recorder, low D whistle
Recorded in Roy Harper's home studio in Ireland
Chris Thorpe: mastering
Harry Pearce: cover design

Roy lives near Clonakilty in Ireland, overlooking the moors. There is a large stone built into his living room wall, which is likely to have come from a nearby stone circle.

The Green Man is a pagan fertility god. A symbol of nature rebirth, the spirit is clothed in the green leaves of renewal. He is often represented by a man sprouting leaves or peering through a circle of foliage.

The album's theme is that we are part of something so much more, though it is a return to basics. Roy decided to dispense with a rhythm section and play acoustic guitar, just like in the old days. The bulk of songs were recorded solo or with Jeff Martin accompanying. Roy's tracks were recorded in one take. The album cover – designed by Harry Pearce – depicts Roy as the Green Man, peering through the foliage.

'The Green Man'

It's an atmospheric start. The guitar work is extraordinary and resonant, generating a mesmeric melody with an underlying hum. Roy's rich voice overlays the guitar with a stratum of poetry.

He's been interested in death and rebirth since childhood. Regeneration has been a recurring theme in his work. Nature is regenerative, but humans are likely to have only a fleeting existence. The Green Man is the eternal spirit: nature renewing itself. Nature was here before us, and it will be here when we are gone. Roy is drawn to our old religion: a pagan worship of nature, in harmony with the planet. He resents the intrusion of the imported Abrahamic traditions (Christianity, Judaism and Islam). He sees these religions as contrived and controlling, pulling us away from the mystery of nature.

This song contains many myths associated with the woodland and moors of Rossmore. The rolling fog creates a low-lying sea in which the mystic prevails and the past and future merge.

'Wishing Well'

A second acoustic piece of digital dexterity. The pipes interact finely as the song develops. It continues the theme of pagan religion. As usual, the poetry is multi-layered and open to interpretation. Roy sings of the relationship with his woman, with love, with nature, the planet, and the pagan forces that flow through us. He is reflecting on the way the balance has moved from one of harmony with nature, to one of abuse, greed and destruction. He is remembering how it had once been and how we have destroyed so much of what was good.

The hawthorn with May blossom represents healing and hope.

'Sexy Woman'

This is somewhat unusual. Jeff Martin's slide guitar gives the sound a harder edge, taking us into a different world. There are all sorts of sounds, from whistles and bongos to keyboards, giving the track drive. It's a real change of mood, with a totally different feel to what has gone before.

The music develops into a groove reflecting the rise of arousal. Lust, attraction and the primaeval urge that drives us are mixed with creation, the planet's biosphere, imagination, contemplation and losing control. It's not so much a love as a lust song – a primitive force of procreation. Heartbeats and musk. Nature is sex.

'The Apology'

An instrumental track with two picking guitars hitting harmonics, while Roy sings 'I am so sorry'. Indecipherable words in lilting tones resound in the background.

'Midnight Sun'

'Midnight Sun' is a gentle love song (with sex), played in Roy's distinctive picking style. It's an intimate expression of love, with a nod to his beloved Nord Cap: home of the midnight sun.

'Glasto'

Now a fast rhythm with an upward feel. Roy is having a blast on this. His words paint pictures of an event: a jaunty tour through the fun of the gathering.

The Glastonbury festival is special, because so many different types of people meet in one huge harmonious bubble. Glastonbury still breeds the atmosphere of energy and togetherness that we used to feel everywhere.

'The Monster'

The album centrepiece. 'The Monster' starts low-key, Roy's vocal sounding like a lament, incredibly true and expressive. The song builds, and once again, the slide guitar provides impetus before a return to a mood of sad helplessness and futility.

Roy is describing the monster that is society. With cash as its religion, this western culture is overwhelming the planet and enslaving the world with a lust to consume: a society from which there is no escape. Politicians are mainly all versions of each other, wedded to the same principle, of wealth before people. Meanwhile, the monster devours everything in its path. The monster we have created has consumed our natural way of life. We are living the apocalypse. It's insane and we're all part of it.

'The Monster' – with its algorithms and superstitions – is a true descendant of 'I Hate The White Man'. It's eight and a half minutes of thought-provoking philosophy. A track to listen to again and again, to ponder and absorb.

'New England'

Now this would've made a worthy single: full of vim, with a catchy chorus and lively backing. The vocal is superb, with a wide range and versatility. Mandolin, piano and bongos, augment the keyboards and interesting guitar rhythms.

But in many ways, the production is at odds with the content. It's an autobiographical romp of rebellion about growing old and passing the baton to the next generation. Roy is observing modern culture's vacuous nature, consumer TV, and life in general with its dichotomy of nationalistic fervour and straitjackets. This was written in the midst of New Labour under Tony Blair, Britpop and Cool Britannia.

'Solar Wind Sculptures'

At the time this song was written, Roy's friend, Ashley Franklin, was a BBC Derby DJ. His daughter, Clare, has Down's syndrome. One day, whilst driving home, she observed and commented that, 'The sky goes all the way home'.

The track has the mood of one of Roy's 1960s songs, like 'Feeling All The Saturday'; jangly guitar, bright, optimistic and delightful. The rhythm feels like a fairground merry-go-round. There's an element of fun and silliness, belying the poetic observations of our planet sculpted through the sun, wind and water of billions of years. The lost chromosome that creates Down's syndrome can also provide an alternative perspective on reality.

'Rushing Camelot'

Lilting recorder and guitar move into a plaintive vocal. The simple arrangement features Uilleann pipes, adding variation, culminating in a circular weaving of voices, 'As we go spinning 'round the world'.

The poem is a plea for a return to a natural way of life in the face of this mad hectic dash towards a synthetic future of genetically modified plants and animals. Roy's despairing vision is of a plastic universe, with everyone watching game shows in a world where money does all the talking. Instead of this rush to an artificial future, should we not walk barefoot in nature and love and really feel the earth move?; Live our lifespan and pass an unspoilt world on to those who follow? We are all too busy 'Rushing Camelot'.

'All In All'

The album ends in a pounding, upbeat guitar extravaganza. The slide guitar
sets you moving, and Roy sings in celebration of life.

It stems from a line of Aldous Huxley's book, *The Doors of Perception*,
that Roy remembered from his youth. Within every moment is everything – a
philosophical notion of perfection. Within nature, within relationship, a perfect
place. It's a strong, positive note to end the album with.

Single – The Death Of God (Long version)/The Death Of God (Short Version) (2005)

Science Friction label 2005
Personnel:
Roy Harper: vocals, guitar, songwriting
Matt Churchill: electric guitar
John Fitzgerald: keyboard
Laurie
Duncan
George Fort: cover design
Brad and Monica: cover design

This strange single – unrelated to any album – was recorded and released in angry response to the Iraq war, including the degrading scenes from Abu Ghraib prison.

One thing was certain: a thirteen-minute-long anti-war song was extremely unlikely to be a hit, no matter how good it was. Not that it bothered Roy. Even the 2m:58s edit wasn't going to make it onto Radio 2, who were none too keen on political or religious themes. We needed another John Peel: a man not averse to playing uncommercial songs, as long as they were good.

Like all Roy's epics, this moves through many phases. With gently-picked guitar and a dreamy vocal, Roy bizarrely sets the scene of watching another Iraq War killing day being played out on TV. He watches, holding his tongue, wondering where this is going. He sees refugees flood away from the theatre of war. The musical mood is sombre but changes as bongos and cool electric guitar appear. An angrier Harper raises the tempo, asking the question: are we just cannon fodder to germinate war? Leaders justify their actions with religious pronouncements. The implication is that beyond the door lies an imaginary realm – Paradise? Heaven? – where the dead will be reunited. This section has Roy's characteristic harmony vocals.

The next section – spoken over a quiet acoustic guitar – describes American guards in Abu Ghraib prison, torturing and humiliating blindfolded prisoners.

The song progresses to an angry conclusion, 'as the suicide bomber, directed by God, blows up innocent people'.

In a more gentle tone, Roy appears as the 'interventionist god', intoning, 'Welcome to the promised land. Sorry I made you kill all those innocent children. They were all warned and fully understand. The innocent children were killed for a reason and will burn in everlasting hell'.

Building to a loud rocking section, Roy intimates that as no weapons of mass destruction were ever found, the whole justification dissolves away, and the fictitious god metaphorically falls out of the sky. The final section builds to a climax.

The thrust of the song is that war – with refugees, soldiers, suicide bombers, leaders and imaginary gods – is a self-perpetuating cycle of violence.

Man And Myth (2013)

Bella Union label 2013
Personnel:
Roy Harper: producer
John Fitzgerald: producer
Jonathan Wilson: producer
Roy Harper: guitar, vocals and all song writing
Jonathan Wilson: banjo, guitar, mandolin, bass guitar and backing vocals
John Fitzgerald: bouzouki, oud, bass guitar, guitar – engineering
Pete Townshend: electric guitar
Tony Franklin: bass guitar
Jake Blanton: bass guitar
Jason Borger: keyboard
Fiona Brice: strings and brass
Gillon Cameron: violin
Bertrand Gale: cello
Richard Gowen: drums and percussion
Justin Grounds: violin
Matt Gunner: horn
George Hart: double bass
Andy Irvine: mandola, bouzouki
James King: alto saxophone
Vicky Matthews: cello
Neal Morgan: percussion
Gabe Noel: cello, double bass
Tom Piggot-Smith: violin
Rachel Robson: viola
Bill Shanley: guitar
Beth Symmons: double bass
Omar Velasco: clavinet and mellotron
Recorded at the FiveStar studio, Echo Park and County Cork
Highest UK chart place: 44

For a long time, it seemed like Roy had stopped recording. 2000's *The Green Man* was his last album. He had, of course, recorded the anti-war epic, 'The Death Of God' in 2005. But apart from that, he was content to stay at home in Ireland: writing poetry, researching history (one of his passions), and occasionally putting together a small tour. His output was limited to compilations and live albums. That was it.

Except, that wasn't it. A new generation of musicians had discovered Roy's genius. Johnny Marr cited *Stormcock* as one of the best ever albums: 'If ever there was a secret weapon of a record, it would be *Stormcock* ... It's intense and beautiful and clever; *Hunky Dory's* big, badder brother'.

Artists in the USA new-folk scene cited him as a major influence. Joanna

Newsom brought Roy out of retirement to tour with her in 2010 when he played *Stormcock* in its entirety. In 2011, US producer, Jonathan Wilson, was a special guest at Roy's 70th birthday Royal Festival Hall celebration concert. And, of course, he was receiving great praise from the press.

In 2010, UK artist, Richard Grayson, produced a 63-minute film focussing on Roy interviews, titled *The Magpie Index*: a single-screen, high-definition video artwork:

> The Magpie Index explores the ways that a fierce personal vision has developed and how this might have shaped the belief systems of a cultural movement. The work moves from the biographical into the social and cultural spheres, to present this individual voice in ways that allude to the traditions of the radical non-conformist, the visionary and the outsider.

The film was shown at The Baltic Contemporary Centre in Gateshead, Tyne and Wear, and The De La Warr Pavilion in Bexhill, Sussex.

What was going on? The anti-establishment rebel was becoming the flavour of the month. In 2013, the BBC Radio 2 Folk Awards presented Roy with a Lifetime Achievement Award.

The upshot of all this was that Jonathan Wilson coaxed Roy into his Echo Park, CA studio, to record another album: *Man and Myth*. It received glowing reviews, garnering phrases like 'An absolute Corker', 'A triumph' and 'A return to form': all of which must have astounded Roy. He was not used to being courted by the press. An hour-long documentary film, titled *Man and Myth*, was produced in 2013, and shown on Sky Arts.

The Man and Myth album is a quiet, subdued, reflective, and a remarkable feat. Roy's voice is powerful; the music experimental and contemplative; his performance, intense and emotional.

'The Enemy', 'Time Is Temporary', 'The Stranger' and 'Heaven Is Here' were recorded at Jonathan Wilson's Fivestar studios. 'Cloud Cuckooland', 'The Exile', and 'January Man' were recorded at Roy's studio in Ireland. The old connections remain: Pete Townshend plays guitar on 'Cloud Cuckooland'.

'The Enemy'

The album starter is an upbeat number with a chilling message. There are a myriad of instruments, and the production is good, with everything perfectly audible and some great guitar licks. Roy's voice is as clear, expressive and resonant as ever.

The song can be interpreted as a lament for the loss of village communities: places where everyone knew everyone and could see where trouble was coming from. Nowadays – in cities, where people are strangers or on the web with internet hackers and false IDs – life is not safe. We don't know who to trust anymore.

Then there's 'The other side of the sky', where life can be different.

'Time Is Temporary'

A change of style and pace here, as Roy plays an intricate guitar piece with a haunting melody. There is sympathetic orchestration and guitar and banjo joining in a difficult staccato section.

Roy sings a love song for a passing vision of beauty, wondering whether the feeling might be mutual and could develop into something more. But the moment doesn't last. In the metronomic, rhythmic conclusion, there is perhaps a wistful reflection on his long and fruitful life.

'January Man'

The wistful mood continues with a soft guitar track. The emotive and pure vocal reflects a mood of loss, just as the chiming guitar captures the sadness of memories. The orchestration augments this pathos of longing and hurt. Roy is reminiscing with regret, but the sadness is kept at bay as he looks ahead to new love and an emergence from winter.

'The Stranger'

A song in the same mournful vein, though the refrain is melodic and catchy.

Looking in the mirror is a harrowing experience. We never see the image of who we think we are. Looking out from the mirror is the ghost of what might have been. Reminiscent of Robert Frost's poem, 'The Road Not Taken', 'The Stranger' reflects on the loss of possible outcomes. There is a yearning to be back with that choice for one last time. Janus – the god of beginnings – looks forward and back.

Is the ghost in the mirror really Roy? Or is it the someone else he could've been? Is it a glimpse back at two possible versions of himself? What else is there? Who is in that reflection? The one who denied love? The one who left for fortune? Or someone else?

'Cloud Cuckooland'

There is nothing quiet, subdued or reflective about this angry polemic of vitriolic acrimony. The band hammers the message home in a gutsy display of classic rock fervour, complete with guitar courtesy of Pete Townsend (obviously enjoying himself), plus some great saxophone from James King. This track blows out all the cobwebs as Roy takes a swipe at modern culture and the shallowness and exploitative immorality devouring the world. Imported American squealing, game shows, bankers and the elite, greedy arms dealers and hypocritical politicians all get a mention. We are condemned to live in a debauched cuckoo land that is destroying the planet and enslaving us in its utter trivial mindlessness. Roll on Armageddon so the world can start again, or not.

This is Roy back to his best, doing what he does well: taking on our 'great' society. It's the album's most rumbustious song and probably my favourite.

'Heaven Is Here'

Roy now launches into a myth comparing humanity's voyage of discovery with his own personal journey. This fifteen-and-a-half-minute epic requires full concentration. It passes through many phases and sections, the poetic lyrics heavily disguised with many references that require decoding. The song is a Homeric odyssey.

In his youth, Roy was surely an Argonaut on a reckless voyage, mirroring mankind's early ventures. The lyric is about the age of heroic discovery and hard-won truth, wherein the Golden Fleece represents power and kingship.

There are many allusions. Eurydice – the nymph wife of Orpheus the musician – died from a snakebite. Orpheus journeyed through the underworld to charm the god, Hades, with his playing, to persuade Hades to release Eurydice. But Orpheus cast a backward glance before they were clear, and Eurydice was lost. This theme of loss and hope pervades most of the album.

The references continue. *The Golden Bough* – a book on the study of religion – spanned from fertility, rituals, magic and religion, through to scientific belief. Then we have the snake in the tale of Eurydice: or is it the snake from the Adam and Eve story? Is it a metaphor for the birth of religion and how that destroyed the innocence of our harmony with nature? The lyric reflects both the loss of love and the loss of our natural way of life.

Selene is the moon Goddess. Perhaps she will wake us from this nightmare.

Having chosen a wide canvas on which to paint his words, Roy set about embellishing them with musical colour. This resulted in instrumentation and dynamics, worthy of his greatest work.

The piece starts with Roy strumming guitar, his voice is relaxed as he relates the tale. Gradually the fretless bass builds with a splash of percussion and deployment of harmonies before the orchestration comes in. The Eurydice section, played with picked guitar, strings and percussion, gives way to ominous strumming as the world and love are lost. The piece softens as Roy's voice pleads with an operatic touch and the guitar picks through the reflection and guilt. Is Roy responsible for the loss? Are we all responsible?

Is this the moment we should have woken?

The percussion comes in as the rhythm changes. The guitar strums faster through an instrumental section that gradually builds before subsiding back to Roy and a picked guitar as he sings of lying and plundering politicians.

The rhythm picks up again and percussion builds as Roy contemplates the truth that has been lost.

Then, plaintive guitar followed by strings and percussion as Roy's voice rises and the track fades on a long drawn out note behind which Roy's voice can only just be discerned.

'Heaven Is Here' is an epic that sees Roy exploring myth, comparing it to the depths of his own emotional experience.

'The Exile'

I wanted to laugh. I had a picture in my head of Roy as a forlorn decapitated lover, exiled and washed up on a distant island as an oracle.

The continuation of the myth is seven and a half highly atmospheric minutes, starting with an eerie sound, drifting guitar notes and a steady rhythm. Roy asserts that life is eternal, as is death. Exiled from love, we are all doomed to look back; removed from the life we might have had. Orpheus is indeed universal. We are exiled from ourselves.

It's a suitable track to finish on, as Roy adds a final coda – forever lost.

Live Recordings and Radio Sessions

Flashes From The Archives Of Oblivion (1974)

First released on the Harvest label in 1974
Personnel:
Pete Jenner: producer
Roy Harper: vocals, guitar and all songwriting
Jimmy Page: guitar on 'Male Chauvinist Pig Blues', 'Too Many Movies' and 'Home' (live version)
Keith Moon: drums on 'Male Chauvinist Pig Blues' and 'Too Many Movies'
Ronnie Lane: bass on 'Male Chauvinist Pig Blues', 'Home' and 'Too Many Movies'
Ian Anderson: flute on 'Home' studio version
David Bedford: orchestral arrangement
John Leckie: sound engineer
Recorded live at various locations

This was released as a double live album, recorded at various venues, including The Royal Albert Hall and The Rainbow Theatre. The cover photo – featuring Roy virtually naked, wearing only Manchester City socks with pants pulled down, flashing, nearly caused the Hayes production factory ladies to walk out. A compromise was reached, with a large black circle placed over the offending member. In the 1980s, Roy had the missing member reproduced as a circular stick-on patch so that people could see the album restored to its original glory.

The album contains songs from *Flat Baroque And Berserk*, *Stormcock*, *Lifemask*, *Valentine*, and two new tracks. Roy's live act at that time usually comprised just him on acoustic guitar, with few frills, soundboard magic or other backing, although the Rainbow Theatre recordings feature The Intergalactic Elephant Band of Jimmy Page, Keith Moon and Ronnie Lane. The one studio track is 'Home', with the Intergalactic band and Jethro Tull's Ian Anderson on flute.

The album has John Leckie's work all over it. The completely reworked 'Highway Blues' is slower; 'Another Day' is orchestral; 'Twelve Hours Of Sunset' features Roy on his twelve-string guitar, and 'Me And My Woman' is actually 'better' than the *Stormcock* version. The album captures Roy at his acoustic best.

Track listing:

'Home' (studio version – full band)
'Commune'
'Don't You Grieve'
'Twelve Hours Of Sunset'
'Kangaroo Blues'
'All Ireland'
'Me And My Woman'
'South Africa'
'Highway Blues'

'One Man Rock And Roll Band'
'Another Day'
'Male Chauvinist Pig Blues' (acoustic with Jimmy Page)
'Too Many Movies' (The Intergalactic Elephant Band)
'Home' (Live version – The Intergalactic Elephant Band)

The two new tracks are 'Home' (two versions) and 'Kangaroo Blues'. The album offers a full spectrum of love songs and powerful, angry epics. On certain numbers, delay and reverb were effectively deployed to create sound layers that filled the auditorium, sounding like a whole army of Harpers (Listen to the great version of 'Highway Blues').

In 1989, the album was re-released as a single CD on Awareness Records. Due to CD time constraints, three tracks were dropped – 'Home (studio version)'; 'Too Many Movies' (which was not the song's best recording anyway), and 'Home (live)'. But these three dropped songs were incongruously included as bonus tracks on the 1989 Awareness reissue of *Valentine*.

Somewhere, there must exist quality recordings of all the concert performances from which this album was culled!

'Kangaroo Blues'

That's Nick Harper calling out for 'Kangaroo Blues' at the beginning. It was recorded in The Royal Albert Hall. This was the only version of the song that existed until an updated version from the Blair/Bush era. The song uses humour to mask social comment.

Roy starts in operatic a cappella, with sexually provocative lyrics containing oblique religious and political references. With punchy guitar chords, he launches into a dig at politicians and society in general, along the way having a go at Nixon, Heath, and the very premise of our civilisation. It ends with the anarchist statement that, there 'ain't no rules that can ever be right'.

Like most of us in that cold war period, Roy felt jumpy about society. Not only were we (the 1960s alternative community) aware that we had a dozen nuclear missiles aimed at us, but society itself was in a mad rush to destroy and control, with a mantra of 'growth, growth, growth'. We were opposed to everything that stood for. We were the outsiders, and society was at war with us.

At the end of the song, Roy would hop off the stage like a kangaroo.

'Home'

This was another attempt at a single, hence its rather poppy, catchy sing-along chorus. The studio version features Jethro Tull's Ian Anderson on flute. It rocks along but lacks any gravitas. It is what it is. The album could well have done without it (as the CD release did).

The live version is from the 1974 Valentine's Day Massacre concert featuring The Intergalactic Elephant Band of Roy, Jimmy Page, Keith Moon and Ronnie Lane. It's very rough and ready, but much more fun!

Single
'Home' b/w 'Home' (Live)
Both tracks were taken from the album.

On 31 August 1974, Roy brought together another Supergroup for a one-off free concert in Hyde Park. This time the line-up was Dave Gilmour (Pink Floyd) on lead guitar, John Paul Jones (Led Zeppelin) on bass, and Steve Broughton (Edgar Broughton Band) on drums. They performed three numbers: 'Highway Blues', 'Me And My Woman' and the sparkling new 'The Game'. This was to auger in the changes we would hear on the next album. Roy was going for a much rockier style.

In Between Every Line (1986)
EMI 1986
Personnel:
Roy Harper: producer
Roy Harper: guitar, vocals, keyboards, saxophone and all songwriting
Nick Harper: guitar
Jimmy Page: guitar
Steve Broughton: drums, guitar, keyboards, vocal
Tony Franklin: bass
Nik Green: keyboards, synthesiser
Robin Ayling: production
Recorded at many live venues – including the 1984 Cambridge Folk Festival – over 18 months into 1985

Track listing:
'One Of Those Days In England' (Solo with ovation guitar)
'Short And Sweet' (Harper, Gilmour) (With band and Jimmy Page)
'Referendum' (With band and Jimmy Page)
'Highway Blues' (With band and Jimmy Page)
'True Story' (With band)
'The Game' (Acoustic with Nick Harper)
'One Man Rock And Roll Band' (Solo with ovation guitar)
'Hangman' (Solo)

Following the success of *Whatever Happened To Jugula?*, EMI came back on board, offering another contract. Their first venture in this new relationship was a double live album. Roy was doing many gigs with Jimmy Page, and EMI obviously thought this would help give a boost. They wanted to build on the success of Jugula, viewing Roy once more as a viable proposition.

At the time, I was working with Roy on a book of lyrics. I suggested a working title of Off The Tracks And Between The Lines. I think that had an influence on this album's title.

Many gigs were recorded, including The Cambridge Folk Festival 1984, where Roy played with Jimmy. When it came to selecting the tracks and sorting between all the different gigs' versions, everything became mixed up. In the end, nobody was really sure which track came from which gig, eventually deciding that it didn't really matter.

With no new songs, the material is a range from *Stormcock*, *Lifemask*, *HQ* and *The Unknown Soldier* – though interestingly, nothing from *Jugula*. What we do have is a double album of outstanding tracks – every one of them a live gem.

Snippets of Roy's crowd banter were kept in, showing the warmth and repartee between artist and audience. At this time, he was developing an electronic presentation to enhance his performance: pedals and effects becoming an integral part of the act. With the help of Jacqui on the mixing desk (a work of art in itself), each song became a sophisticated soundscape. To hear how one man with his guitar could create such a wall of sound was amazing. At times it seemed like Roy had morphed into Phil Spector and was indeed that one-man rock and roll band.

The Roy Harper Band (Tony Franklin, Nik Green, Steve Broughton) features on a number of tracks. Working within the group confines restricted Roy's innate idiosyncrasies, requiring him to be more controlled. Despite his inbuilt quirkiness, the band worked remarkably well together.

At various gigs, Jimmy Page joined in, making for an acoustic duo, moving to electric guitar with the band. Jimmy added interest and took the music to a different dimension. Sadly, none of their shared acoustic performances made it onto the album.

Roy's son, Nick, was also an ideal foil for the former's guitar work. The two formed a formidable acoustic duo (as heard on 'The Game), which put Nick on the first rung of his own career.

The album is a superb glimpse into the extensive musical world of Harper in the mid-1980s: a progressive act who had travelled a long way since his first album. The sophisticated production and musicianship are on another level. It was released on CD in 1994, through Roy's Science Friction label – although, in order to fit the format, 'Hangman' was sacrificed. Unfortunately, *In Between Every Line* did not repeat the success of *Jugula*.

Live At The Red Lion: Birmingham visits I-III (1990)

In 1990, Roy's 'management' released semi-official tapes of solo performances at Birmingham's Red Lion. There were no new songs in the three sets, but the arrangements and scope of material were tremendous. The sound quality was good; the sets a snapshot of Roy's repertoire and stagecraft in the mid-1980s. What is particularly revealing is his intimate relationship with the audience: the exchanges and relaxed repartee are warm. They were not so much concerts, as gatherings.

Birmingham 1984 (First visit)
Side A:
'Tom Tiddler's Ground'
'One Man Rock And Roll Band'
'Me And My Woman'
'I Hate The White Man'

Side B:
'Highway Blues'
'Elizabeth'
'Hangman'
'When An Old Cricketer Leaves The Crease'
'North Country'

1984 (Second visit)
Side A:
'South Africa'
'Hallucinating Light'
'Don't You Grieve'
'Highway Blues'
'Commune'
'Frozen Moment'
'20th Century Man'

Side B:
'I Hate The White Man'
'Another Day'
'One Of Those Days In England'
'Hangman'

1985 (Third Visit)
Side A:
'Commune'
'Don't You Grieve'
Frozen Moment'
'20th Century Man'
'I Hate The White Man'
'North Country'

Side B:
'One Of Those Days In England'
'Hangman'

Live At Les Cousins (1996)
Blueprint Label 1996
Personnel:
Roy Harper: producer, vocals, guitar and all songwriting
Peter Sarner: engineer
Recorded on EMI Mobile Recording Studio Live at Les Cousins, 49 Greek Street,
Soho
Darren Crisp: mastering and cover design
Opher Goodwin: liner notes (and provision of photo)

This concert was recorded on 30 August 1969, the day before Bob Dylan
performed at the Isle of Wight festival. I had the choice and decided on Les
Cousins.

Roy had wanted to record 'I Hate The White Man' live in front of his own
crowd, for *Flat Baroque And Berserk*. He had learnt a lesson from the earlier
'McGoohan's Blues' recording and wanted this centrepiece to be live and full
of energy and anger. He chose Les Cousins because that was where he had
started out, and it was now his second home. It was an intimate venue and
would generate exactly the vibe he was looking for.

He managed to persuade EMI – his new label – to set up their mobile
recording unit, and all was set. News of the gig had circulated quickly amongst
the faithful fans, and I remember the place was packed, hot and smoky. There
was a great buzz. It cost five shillings to get in! I was there early, sat at a table
close to the stage. The atmosphere was electric.

Fortunately for us, the entire gig was taped, and those tapes lay in the EMI
vaults until the mid-1990s when Roy managed to gain control of his material
that EMI held. Only four of the tapes were found, with one was missing.

Darren Crisp – Roy's manager (an impossible task) – mastered the tapes with
Chris Thorpe at Serendipity Studios. I provided the back cover photo: taken at
Barking College in September 1968, by a photographer whose name I cannot
remember. He gave me a couple of large black and white prints because he
knew I was such a Harper fan. I also had the privilege of writing the liner notes.

It's fascinating to see the album's range of material. Roy was playing numbers
from *Sophisticated Beggar, Come Out Fighting Ghengis Smith, Folkjokeopus,*
and the single, 'Zengem', along with new numbers that would appear on
Flat Baroque And Berserk. He even played songs that wouldn't surface until
Stormcock or Valentine. I'd forgotten that 'Hors D'Oeuvres' and 'Che' dated
back to that time.

Disc 1
'You Don't Need Money'
'North Country'
'Hors D'Oeuvres'
'Blackpool'

'She's The One' (String change)
'She's The One'
'Goldfish'
'East Of The Sun'

Disc 2
'McGoohan's Blues'
'Feeling All The Saturday'
'Zengem'
'Che'
'Davey'
'I Hate The White Man'
'Goodbye'
'Tom Tiddler's Ground' (Edit – the tape came to an end)

I'm glad that all the gig talk was left in. An essential element of a Harper gig is the stuff in between the songs. All the tracks feature Roy, his acoustic guitar and microphone; no pedals, effects or other instrumentation. Brilliant. Not that I dislike the later effects and production – it's just good to hear Roy as he was at that time. A snapshot of history.

The BBC Tapes I-VI (1997)
Science Friction label

Along with rights ownership of all his EMI albums and the Les Cousins tapes, Roy also gained the rights to all his BBC recordings of the period. They were mastered and put out as six CDs. There are some brilliant performances.

BBC Tapes – Vol I
This album features Roy with just an acoustic guitar and harmonica.

Top Gear (1969)
John Walters: producer
Roy Harper: acoustic guitar, harmonica, vocals and all songwriting

There are some interesting features on these live recordings. 'Francesca' has Superb fingerpicking. 'Hell's Angels' is played solo with a wah-wah pedal on the guitar, and there's a great version of 'She's The One'. 'I Hate The White Man' has a squeak at the beginning and is a little restrained. There's also a rare outing for the harmonica, on 'It's Tomorrow And Today Is Yesterday'.

1. 'Francesca'
2. 'Hell's Angels'
3. 'She's The One'

4. 'I Hate The White Man'
5. 'It's Tomorrow And Today Is Yesterday'

Top Gear (1970)

John Walters: producer
Roy Harper: acoustic guitar, vocals and all songwriting

'Don't You Grieve' is a straight run through. 'I Hate The White Man' is
superb. 'North Country' is rather spoilt for me, by a piss-take of Dylan, at the
beginning.

6. 'Don't You Grieve'
7. 'I Hate The White Man'
8. 'North Country'

Bob Harris Session (1973)

Pete Ritzema: producer
Bill Aikin: engineer
Roy Harper: acoustic guitar, vocals and all songwriting

There is a lot of synthesizer and added production on these recordings.
'Forever' is a deft performance with amazing musicianship. 'Twelve Hours Of
Sunset' has incredible use of the bass strings to create effects. 'South Africa'
exhibits some extraordinary guitar work but has strange stereo vocals and
production that don't quite work (Roy is always one for experimenting).
'Little Lady' has interesting chords, and there appears to be a synthesizer
on the track. 'All Ireland' is a great version, with harmonica tastefully in the
background.

9. 'Forever'
10. 'Twelve Hours Of Sunset'
11. 'South Africa'
12. 'Little Lady'
13. 'All Ireland'

In Concert (1971)

Roy Harper: acoustic guitar, vocals and all songwriting

I don't know where these tapes came from, but they sound rather muffled with
an intrusive background hiss. There must be a superior source because I'm
certain I've heard better quality versions.
    In between 'One Man Rock And Roll Band' and 'The Same Old Rock', Roy
castigates the BBC: 'Everything I don't stand for, now surrounds me. I offer it a
prayer'. I can't imagine this endeared him to the producer.

There is an interesting version of 'Kangaroo Blues'. The sexually explicit intro is skipped (I'm not sure he would've gotten away with it) and the lyric is changed: it's now Reagan and Wayne killing all the 'Injuns'.

14. 'Hors D'Oeuvres'
15.'One Man Rock And Roll Band'
16. 'Same Old Rock'
17. 'Kangaroo Blues'

BBC Tapes – Vol II
Roy Harper: acoustic guitar, vocals and all songwriting (apart from 'North Country')
David Bedford: strings
In Concert – from The Hippodrome, Golders Green, London – 1974.

These recordings have superb sound quality with a great balance and bright guitar sound. Roy plays solo. David Bedford's strings join for the second half, adding another dimension.

I always think Roy feels inhibited when recording for radio or performing with a band or orchestra. This inhibition constrains his performance and stops him from opening out. But this is an unusually relaxed concert.

'Hors D'Oeuvres' has an echo, and after a slightly iffy start, it finally gets into the groove. 'Too Many Movies' is interesting, displaying Roy's atmospheric rhythms.

'Male Chauvinist Pig Blues' gets a rare solo outing. It's a little strange to hear it without the second guitar. Roy has to work harder, and the vocal sounds a tad strained. He works on his audience rapport with some Monty-Python-style gooning-around.

'Forever' is just delightful, and he nails it. 'South Africa', with intricate guitar, is sublime. 'Highway Blues' is dedicated to Bonzo. The driving guitar really gets it going, and the delay pedal comes in again to broaden the sound.

The orchestral accompaniment on 'I'll See You Again' melds well. David Bedford is sympathetic to the music, and Roy is beautifully controlled. 'Commune' showcases another piece of superb picking, augmented with wonderful strings. On the masterpiece, 'Another Day', the vocal sounds a little off at first, but gets better as it goes along. 'North Country' is very good delivered with the strings, although I have heard Roy sing it better. 'Twelve Hours Of Sunset' is impeccable, capturing that dreamy state perfectly.

This concert was previously bootlegged as *Heavy Crazy*, and was popular among Harper fans. The CD was edited, leaving in some dialogue concerning a note a friend had written Roy, telling him to steer clear of politics and not slag off the BBC. Sound advice for a live BBC performance! The slightly dodgy 'Hors D'Oevres' was omitted. To my ears, Heavy Crazy' has a warmer sound than the BBC recordings. I think I prefer the bootleg.

1. 'Hors D'Oeuvres'
2. 'Too Many Movies'
3. 'Male Chauvinist Pig Blues'
4. 'Forever'
5. 'South Africa'
6. 'Highway Blues'
7. 'I'll See You Again'
8. 'Commune'
9. 'Another Day'
10. 'North Country' (Trad.)
11. 'Twelve Hours of Sunset'

BBC Tapes – Vol III
John Peel – Top Gear (1974)
John Waters: producer
Roy Harper: acoustic guitar, vocals and all songwriting (except 'North Country' (Trad.))

This is also a solo session. The recording is excellent, Roy sounding relaxed and in good voice, as he gives stunning deliveries of the love songs, 'Commune' and 'Forever'. I don't think there's a note missed. 'Highway Blues' drives along, Roy pouring his passion in, using some delay to add depth and power.

He then slows it down for 'I'll See You Again'. He has a few minor lyric stumbles, but they are covered up well. 'North Country' is just how it should be sung: with warmth and tenderness. 'Too Many Movies' is another great delivery, with exactly the right amount of delay to create the required atmosphere. It's a nigh-on perfect session.

1. 'Commune'
2. 'Forever'
3. 'Highway Blues'
4. 'I'll See You Again'
5. 'North Country'
6. 'Too Many Movies'

Bob Harris Session (1974)
Pete Ritzema: producer
Roy Harper: acoustic guitar, vocals and all songwriting

This is a great session, but unfortunately, with only two songs. Roy was in good form and we could have done with a few more. It has a slightly warmer quality than the John Peel sessions, but on the whole, I prefer the John Peel.

7. 'Forever'
8. 'North Country'

John Peel Session (1973)
Tony Wilson: producer
Roy Harper: acoustic guitar, vocals and all songwriting

This is another great Peel session, featuring a superb version of 'Highway Blues', with Roy deploying an electric acoustic. The riffs and rhythms motor along, and there's a great middle-eight where he plays an electrifying solo: he really gives it some welly.

'Twelve Hours Of Sunset' is also immaculate. I like the spacey production. That ending sends shivers through me. 'One Man Rock And Roll Band' has everything: fantastic chords, effects, and a perfect vocal. I didn't even miss the second guitar.

The session is topped off with a brilliant 'Too Many Movies'. He even makes 'Home' sound good. This is the best version I've heard of the rather average song. Those Peel sessions are exceptional.

9. 'Highway Blues'
10. 'Twelve Hours Of Sunset'
11. 'One Man Rock And Roll Band'
12. 'Too Many Movies'
13. 'Home'

BBC Tapes – Vol IV
Jeff Griffin: producer
Roy Harper: acoustic guitar, vocals and all songwriting
Chris Spedding: lead guitar
Dave Cochran: bass
Bill Bruford: drums

I think the introduction clearly reveals Roy's mental state at this point. Though the top musicians of the era lauded him, the critics castigated him and he suffered public indifference. The records were not selling well. Roy was feeling despondent, unappreciated, underrated and unloved.

This is a quality live recording of what was a superb band, even if it doesn't really capture how brilliant they were in the small clubs. 'Hallucinating Light' is slightly iffy but still good. The band really hits its stride with 'Referendum': that heavy riff allowing them to let rip. Chris Spedding's lead guitar is brilliant, and the whole atmosphere comes to life.

This is the strangest version of 'Highway Blues' I've ever heard. They've made it into a different song altogether: much slower and more laid-back than I would've imagined from this band. It takes some getting used to but is well worth the effort, even if Roy's voice does go off towards the end.

The band version of 'Too Many Movies' is moody and excellent. 'The Spirit Lives' starts with Roy and guitar. The band entering, at first simmering, then rousing in passion. Guitarist, Spedding, certainly adds a bluesy feel.

'Home' provides some light entertainment. The band is on top of the performance: it's not as ramshackle as the Intergalactic Elephant Band version.

'The Game' is the concert centrepiece. The band is spot on, though Roy's voice is not as good as usual and a little off-key at times.

'Grown Ups Are Just Silly Children' is a super piece of madness to end the gig. I think Roy is doing his Elvis impersonation here.

All told, I felt that this performance was under par for Roy and the band. There are some great sections and a historic memento, but it's not their best.

In Concert – from the Paris Theatre, London – 1975 with Trigger

1. 'Hallucinating light'
2. 'Referendum'
3. 'Highway Blues'
4. 'Too Many Movies'
5. 'The Spirit Lives'
6. 'Home'
7. 'The Game'
8. 'Grown Ups Are Just Silly Children'

BBC Tapes – Vol V
John Peel Session – 1975 with Trigger
Tony Wilson: producer
Roy Harper: acoustic guitar, vocals and all songwriting
Chris Spedding: lead guitar
Dave Cochran: bass
Bill Bruford: drums
Bob Conduct: engineer

Trigger was a really hard-hitting rock band of the first order, and this set reaffirms their superb rock standing. In my opinion, it is superior to the set from the Paris Theatre.

There's a fascinating rendering of 'Hallucinating Light'. The song transfers to a rock setting very well. 'The Spirit Lives' continues the trend, and Roy is in top form. Once again, Chris Spedding plays a searing solo, offering a different dimension. 'Referendum' is another great version. It's a shame there are only three tracks. Roy and the band were perfect.

1. 'Hallucinating Light'
2. 'The Spirit Lives'
3. 'Referendum'

John Peel Session – 1977 with Chips
Tony Wilson: producer
Roy Harper: acoustic guitar, vocals and all songwriting

Dave Lawson: keyboards
John Halsey: drums
Henry McCullough: guitar
Andy Roberts: guitar

Contrary to his recent Paris Theatre announcement, Roy did not disappear off into the distance. He formed another rock band. Chips were less hard-hitting than Trigger – mainly because they lacked Chris Spedding's blues-drenched playing – but were a tad more sophisticated. They took folk-rock to another level.

Here there's a sympathetic electric version of 'Another Day' that loses none of its sensitivity and gentleness. Roy seems completely at home. 'Cherishing The Lonesome' receives the same treatment: the band is really tight, and Roy's vocal, perfect. I loved Trigger, but I think Chips proved to be less demanding on Roy's voice. He does not appear to be straining. This band is versatile and expressive, which suited his style.

The slower numbers, like 'These Last Days', really shine. The band fills the sound out without swamping it. 'Grown Ups Are Just Silly Children' has a hilarious start, receiveing a very different treatment, with prominent keyboards.

It's a great set, from a highly proficient band at the top of its game, and all of them are so obviously enjoying it.

4. 'Another Day'
5. 'Cherishing The Lonesome'
6. 'These Last Days'
7. 'Grown Ups Are Just Silly Children'

John Peel Session – 1978 with Andy Roberts
Tony Wilson: producer
Roy Harper: acoustic guitar, vocals and all songwriting
Andy Roberts: guitar

Roy and Andy bring 'Forget Me Not' to life. Although it is not one of my favourite love songs, this is the best version I've heard. The pair's guitar interplay on 'The Same Old Rock' is simply exquisite and perhaps even better than Roy with Jimmy Page (an amazing feat). Instead of the bluesy Page version, Andy here brings a more Spanish flavour. He coaxes a ringing tone from his guitar. I think this is a faultless performance.

I'm not sure 'I Hate The White Man' is quite as successful. Nevertheless, the performance is masterful and brings a different interpretation.

A superb session.

8. 'Forget Me Not'
9. 'The Same Old Rock'
10. 'I Hate The White Man'

BBC Tapes – Vol VI
In Concert – 1978 with Andy Roberts
Jeff Griffin: producer
Roy Harper: acoustic guitar, vocals and all songwriting
Andy Roberts: guitar

Having seen Roy and Andy at a number of gigs, and after hearing the last
Peel session, I was expecting this to be a brilliant performance, and it
doesn't disappoint. Andy's musicianship is exceptional, and the pair really
gel. Although there is some slight vocal distortion, it doesn't distract too
much.

'Forget Me Not' is even better than in the previous session. There's a
consummate, extraordinary and faultless performance of 'One Of Those Days
In England (Parts 2-10)'. Andy strengthens Roy's delivery in the choruses.
Then comes a great version of 'I Hate The White Man', if a little restrained.
'The Same Old Rock' continues with the pair's tremendous rapport.

'Twelve Hours Of Sunset' is sung in an appropriately relaxed manner. The
echo works its magic as a dreamy melding of time and space takes place.
'Highway Blues' is a fitting track to end with.

The power of two brilliant musicians is fully realised. They really are a two-
man rock and roll band.

1. 'Forget me not'
2. 'One Of Those Days In England (Parts 2-10)'
3. 'I Hate The White Man'
4. 'The Same Old Rock'
5. 'Twelve Hours Of Sunset'
6. 'Highway Blues'

These six CDs are packed with live goodies, unusual arrangements and a
variety of presentations: both acoustic and electric. They illuminate the scope
of Roy's music and range of styles. But above that, they are documents of
specific periods in time: historic milestones in his career.

Royal Festival Hall (2001)
Science Friction label
Personnel:
Roy Harper: producer
Roy Harper: vocals, guitar and all songwriting (apart from 'North Country' (Trad.)
and 'Key To The Highway' (Big Bill Broonzy)
David Bedford and the Bedford Strings: orchestration
Troy Dunockley: uilleann pipes
Andy Roberts: acoustic guitar
Nick Harper: acoustic guitar

Jeff Martin: acoustic guitar
John Renbourn: acoustic guitar
Ric Sanders: fiddle
Tony Pugh: engineer
Darren Crisp: design
Peter Jenner: organisation

The concert on 10 June 2001 was an early celebration of Roy's 60th birthday on 12 June. There was certainly a party atmosphere and a fabulous ambience in the Royal Festival Hall. The audience were exhilarated. Nobody (including Roy) had expected him to reach 60. His life had been packed with excess, and following a serious medical condition (hemorrhagic telangiectasia), it had looked unlikely he would live into his 60s and beyond – but he did. He was still going strong and is now – 20 years later – planning a similar event to celebrate his 80th birthday.

Roy assembled a notable group of suitable rascals to support him. There was John Renbourn: his friend from his 1960s days at Les Cousins; David Bedford: string arranger for albums like *Stormcock*; Andy Roberts of Black Sheep, who Roy had also toured with as a duo; Jeff Martin of The Tea Party; Ric Sanders of Soft Machine and Fairport Convention; Troy Dunockley who had worked with Roy in Ireland; and last but not least, Roy's son, Nick Harper. For contractual reasons, Jimmy Page could not play but watched from a box and gave support.

The stage was set for a superb evening and that's what we had. The various collaborations begat an unusual performance, the warm reception visibly moving Roy; especially when just prior to 'Key To The Highway', the entire audience broke into a rousing rendition of 'Happy Birthday'.

All the songs were Roy's, except for 'Key To The Highway' – an old Big Bill Broonzy blues number from Roy's busking days – on this occasion featuring the great John Renbourn. The song is a tale of parting and life on the road. It was the first time Roy and John had played together since the mid-1960s. They continued with 'Sophisticated Beggar': the original version of which John had played second guitar on. All very nostalgic.

The concert was recorded and released as a double CD.

Disc 1
1. 'Commune' – with David Bedford and the Bedford strings
2. 'I'll See You Again' – with David Bedford and the Bedford strings
3. 'Rushing Camelot' – with Troy Donockley
4. 'North Country' (Trad.) – with David Bedford and the Bedford strings
5. 'Another Day' – with Andy Roberts, and David Bedford and the Bedford strings
6. 'Hallucinating Light' – with Nick Harper
7. 'Same Old Rock' – with Nick Harper

Disc 2
8. 'Sexy Woman' – with Jeff Martin
9. 'Key To The Highway' (Broonzy) – with John Renbourn
10. 'Sophisticated Beggar' – with John Renbourn
11. 'Highway Blues' – with Nick Harper and Ric Sanders
12. 'Twelve Hours Of Sunset' – with David Bedford and the Bedford strings
13. 'Me And My Woman' – with Nick Harper, and David Bedford and the Bedford strings
14.'The Flycatcher' – with Andy Roberts and Nick Harper
15. 'The Green Man'

Beyond The Door (2005)
Science Friction label
Personnel:
Roy Harper: producer
Roy Harper: vocals, guitar and all songwriting
Matt Churchill: guitar
John Fitzgerald: keyboards (DVD track 8), sound recording
Duncan Lutz: bass (DVD track 8)
Laurie Hedger: percussion (DVD track 8)
Jon Mitton: editor, art direction (Video) and authoring
Ian Armstrong: film director
John O'Donahue: sound recording
Recorded at the De Barras Folk Club in June 2004

Beyond The Door was Roy's first DVD release. Filmed around his home in Ireland, it contains some candid Harper-isms of the first order. As usual, he is open, full of opinions and revealing of his emotions. There are some interesting songs, including a great updated version of 'Kangaroo Blues' (which has a kick at Blair and Bush). The songs were filmed over three nights at the De Barras Folk Club in Clonakilty. Roy had performed there a number of times and built up a great relationship with the club and audience.

A CD of music from the three live shows went with the DVD. The sound quality is excellent, and the song interpretations are superb.

'Punch And Judy'
The one new track is a poem sung to brightly-picked guitars. It sounds very much like 'Descendants Of Smith', with a metronomic rhythm and great guitar interaction with Matt Churchill. The song employs echo and reverb for a spacey feel.

The song is about a tense relationship. It also deals with mankind's tremendous imagination, which has brought us all manner of inventions. Most have radically improved our lives, but some should never have been invented.

1. 'Tom Tiddler's Ground'
2. 'How Does It Feel'
3. 'Frozen Moment'
4. 'The Green Man'
5. 'Pinches Of Salt'
6. 'One Man Rock And Roll Band'
7. 'Punch And Judy'
8. 'Hallucinating Light'
9. 'Miles Remains'
10. '12 Hours Of Sunset'

Live In Concert At Metropolis Studios, London (2011)
SALVO label 2011
Sinead D'Arcy: producer
Recorded at the Metropolis Studios
Personnel:
Roy Harper: Vocals, guitar and all songwriting
John Fitzgerald: sound engineer

Classic Rock magazine was running a Rock Legends season and turned their attention on Roy. His star was in the ascendency. He was being lauded by a new generation of musicians, including Fleet Foxes, Joanna Newsom and Jeff Martin. Already presented with the 2005 Mojo Hero Award, Roy was in danger of being considered a national treasure. Who could possibly have foreseen that? Certainly not him. But his love song compilations were not controversial. The critics were positive: the music press now seeing him as a major force.

Roy was 70 years old: an age he never thought he would reach. He always said that he would not see old bones, but he was getting there – and getting there in style.

The solo concert took place at West London's Metropolis Studios, in front of a select 120 fans. The intimate affair was recorded and filmed. It was a controlled and perfectly executed performance. I felt emotional watching and listening, thinking back to the hundreds of Harper concerts I'd seen over the years. They had shown a maverick Roy, with raging songs, passion, anarchy, impromptu asides, dialogues, forgotten words, diatribe, and fascinating meanderings and insights. I'd always thrilled as he played selections from his huge lexicon.

The Metropolis concert was equally wonderful but more organised and restrained. This was the grown-up Harper showing he was capable of a mature performance without those earlier anarchistic elements. This was the new Roy, steering clear of anything too controversial without losing his true essence. He was moving into a new phase of his long and productive career.

The set was an interesting mix, spanning his long career. His voice was perhaps a bit lower in register but still intact, expressive and rich in tone. We were no longer 'sitting in his front room', as he aimed for in his early concerts. This was a proper recital.

1 'One Man Rock And Roll Band'
2 'Twelve Hours Of Sunset'
3 'Don't You Grieve'
4 'Another Day'
5 'Pinches Of Salt'
6 'Highway Blues'
7 'Commune'
8 'Hallucinating Light'
9 'Frozen Moment'
10 'The Green Man'
11 'Me And My Woman'
12 'When An Old Cricketer Leaves The Crease'

Compilations

Harper 1970-1975
First released on the Harvest label in 1978
Recorded at Abbey Road studio
Personnel:
Roy Harper: producer
Pete Jenner: producer
Roy Harper: vocals, guitar and all songwriting
Numerous other musicians (see separate albums)

In 1978 EMI released a compilation that is still only available on vinyl. It features tracks from all Roy's Harvest albums. It's far from a 'Best of', but it does demonstrate the strength of the material. Though many of the greatest tracks are missing, it's still a superb album.

1. 'Don't You Grieve' (*Flat Baroque And Berserk*)
2. 'I Hate The White Man' (*Flat Baroque And Berserk*)
3. 'Tom Tiddler's Ground' (*Flat Baroque And Berserk*)
4. 'Me And My Woman' (*Stormcock*)
5. 'Little Lady' (*Lifemask*)
6. 'South Africa' (*Lifemask)*
7. 'Forbidden Fruit' (*Valentine*)
8. 'I'll See You Again' (*Valentine*)
9. 'Commune' (*Valentine*)
10. 'Another Day (Live)' (*Flashes From The Archives Of Oblivion*)
11. 'When An Old Cricketer Leaves The Crease' (*HQ*)
12. 'Home (Studio Version)' (*Flashes From The Archives Of Oblivion*)

An Introduction To (1994)
Science Friction label 1994
Personnel:
Roy Harper: producer
Pete Richard: producer
Shel Talmy: producer
Pete Jenner: producer
Roy Harper: guitar, vocals and all songwriting
Numerous supporting musicians: (For full personnel, see relevant albums)

With his own label – Science Friction – Roy was able to release material how and when he wanted. He has never made a 'Best of' album: the type that might draw in a new audience. The nearest he came to that was Harper 1970-1975. The difficulty is that his best songs are 20-minute epics. A CD would only be room for three! Most people would find it challenging to concentrate on a 20-minute track by an unfamiliar artist.

The decision was made to release something more accessible. It was not so much a 'Best of', as an 'Introduction to', as per the title. The hope was that people might like the taster and then buy another album or two. Consequently, they included one track from each album, with *Death Or Glory?* getting two. Strangely, *Stormcock* does not feature at all (but then, all those tracks are long).

1. 'Legend' (*Sophisticated Beggar*)
2. 'She's The One' (*Folkjokeopus*)
3. 'Tom Tiddler's Ground' (*Flat Baroque And Berserk*)
4. 'Highway Blues' (*Lifemask*)
5. 'Che' (*Valentine*)
6. 'Hallucinating Light' (*HQ*)
7. 'One Of Those Days In England' (*Bullinamingvase*)
8. 'You' (*Unknown Soldier*)
9. 'Nineteen Forty-Eightish' (*Whatever Happened To Jugula?*)
10.' Pinches Of Salt' (*Descendants Of Smith*)
11. 'Ghost Dance' (*Once*)
12. 'The Tallest Tree' (*Death Or Glory?*)
13. 'Miles Remains' (*Death Or Glory?*)

Song Of The Ages (1997)
Science Friction label
A three-CD set of interviews.
CD1 – An introduction to Roy Harper, introduced by Bob Harris, with contributions from Dave Gilmour, Paul McCartney, Ian Anderson and Roy Harper.
CD2 – Radio interviews 1973
CD3 – Radio interviews 1977/1985

Hats Off (2001)
The Right Stuff label (Capitol Records)
Personnel:
Roy Harper: producer
Pete Jenner: producer
Roy Harper: vocals, guitar and all songwriting

This fourteen-song compilation was tailored for the American market. The tracks are culled from different albums, with many songs edited down. It's not so much a 'Best of' as a sampler.

The album title was a reference to the Led Zeppelin III song, 'Hats Off To Roy Harper'. The selling point was the large number of well-known rock stars supporting Roy on the tracks.

The cover looks rather garish and not in Roy's usual artistic style. The album itself is good but is a rather strange concoction.

1. 'Death Or Glory?' – (*Death Or Glory?*)
2. 'Commune' – (*Valentine*)
3. 'Me And My Woman' (Edit) – (*Stormcock*)
4. 'Male Chauvinist Pig Blues' – (*Valentine*)
5. 'Highway Blues' – (*Lifemask*)
6. 'You' – (*The Unknown Soldier*)
7. 'Nineteen Forty-Eightish' (Edit) – (*Whatever Happened To Jugula?*)
8. 'Another Day' (Live) – (*Flashes From The Archives*)
9. 'Don't You Grieve' – (*Flat Baroque And Berserk*)
10. 'Ten Years Ago' – (*Commercial Breaks*)
11. 'These Fifty Years' (Edit) – (*The Dream Society*)
12. 'One Of Those Days In England (Part 1) – (*Bullinamingvase*)
13. 'The Same Old Rock' – (*Stormcock*)
14. 'The Game' (Edit) – (*HQ*)

East Of The Sun (2001)

Science Friction label
Personnel:
Roy Harper: producer
Pete Jenner: producer
Roy Harper: vocals, guitar and all songwriting
Colin Curwood: photography
Harry Pearce: design

This was a turning point. Roy decided to assemble an album of his best love songs. He must've realised that his social commentary epics were only popular with a minority, while his beautifully-crafted love songs had far greater appeal. The resulting collection had nothing that the critics could take umbrage with, and attracted universal acclaim. It was unusual for a Roy Harper album, and signalled a sea change in the way critics viewed him.

East Of The Sun sold well, giving Roy the kind of recognition he had rarely received.

1. 'I'll See You Again' (*Valentine*)
2. 'Francesca' (*Flat Baroque And Berserk*)
3. 'Another Day' (*Flat Baroque And Berserk*)
4. 'North Country' (*Valentine*)
5. 'South Africa' (*Lifemask*)
6. 'The Flycatcher' (*The Unknown Soldier*)
7. 'My Friend' (*Sophisticated Beggar*)
8. 'East Of The Sun' (*Flat Baroque And Berserk*)
9. 'Commune' (*Valentine*)
10. 'Davey' (*Flat Baroque And Berserk*)
11. 'Twelve Hours Of Sunset' (*Valentine*)

12. 'Hallucinating Light' (*HQ*)
13. 'Forever' (*Valentine*)
14. 'Sexy Woman' (*The Green Man*)
15. 'Frozen Moment' (*Whatever Happened To Jugula?*)

Today Is Yesterday (2002)
Science Friction label
Personnel:
Roy Harper: producer
Peter Richards: producer
Shel Talmy: producer
Pete Jenner: producer
Roy Harper: vocals, guitar and all songwriting

This is a compilation of demos and outtakes from the debut, *Sophisticated Beggar*. Also included are two early singles, two *Folkjokeopus* outtakes, and one *Flat Baroque And Berserk* outtake.

It's quite a mishmash of songs, styles and times, with no underlying theme, apart from all tracks being rarities. It's a strange concoction: the track sequence not even chronological.

Tracks 1-9 are the *Sophisticated Beggar* demos, recorded in 1965/1966.

'Pretty Baby' is the B-side of the first single, 'Take Me Into Your Eyes'.

'Midspring Dithering' and 'Zengem' comprised the second single.

'(It's Tomorrow And) Today Is Yesterday' is a *Flat Baroque And Berserk* outtake that was considered as a single but rejected.

'Zaney Janey' and 'Night Fighter (Ballad Of Songwriter)' are *FolkJokeopus* outtakes that were included on the American issue in place of 'One For All'.

'Life Goes By' was the third single.

'Take Me Into Your Eyes' was the first single A-side.

All of these tracks have been described earlier in their relevant chronological place.

1. 'Long Hot Summer Day'
2. 'The Scaffold Of Daylight'
3. 'Black Clouds'
4. 'Girlie'
5. 'In The Morning'
6. 'Love'
7. 'Forever'
8. 'Little Old Lady'
9. 'Mountain'
10. 'Pretty Baby'
11. 'Midspring Dithering'
12. '(It's Tomorrow And) Today Is Yesterday'

13. 'Zengem'
14. 'Zaney Janey'
15. 'Life Goes By'
16. 'Night Fighter' (Ballad Of Songwriter)
17. 'Take Me Into Your Eyes'

Counterculture (2005)

Science Friction label
Personnel:
Roy Harper: producer
Peter Richards: producer
Pete Jenner: producer
Roy Harper: vocals, guitar and all songwriting

Counterculture is another album that could be considered a 'Best of', though it inevitably misses out a number of Roy's greatest songs: no room for 'McGoohan's Blues', 'The Lord's Prayer' or 'The Game'; No 'Forever' or 'How Does It Feel'. We need a box set to do justice to Roy's range and quality. Until then, this will have to do. It probably is the best of the best-ofs.

Disc 1

1. 'Sophisticated Beggar' (*Sophisticated Beggar*)
2. 'You Don't Need Money' (*Come Out Fighting Ghengis Smith*)
3. 'Francesca' *(Flat Baroque and Berserk)*
4. 'I Hate The White Man' (*Flat Baroque and Berserk*)
5. 'Another Day' (*Flashes from the Archives of Oblivion*)
6. 'The Same Old Rock' (*Stormcock*)
7. 'Me And My Woman' (*Stormcock*)
8. 'South Africa' (*Lifemask*)
9. 'I'll See You Again' (*Valentine*)
10. 'Twelve Hours Of Sunset' (*Valentine*)
11. 'Forget Me Not' (*HQ*)
12. 'Hallucinating Light' (*HQ*)
13. 'When An Old Cricketer Leaves The Crease' (*HQ*)

Disc 2

1. 'One Of Those Days In England (Parts 2-10)' (*Bullinamingvase*)
2. 'These Last Days' (*Bullinamingvase*)
3. 'Cherishing The Lonesome' (*Bullinamingvase*)
4. 'The Flycatcher' (*The Unknown Soldier*)
5. 'You' (*The Unknown Soldier*)
6. 'Frozen Moment' (*Whatever Happened to Jugula?*)
7. 'Pinches Of Salt' (*Descendants of Smith*)
8. 'Miles Remains' (*Death or Glory?*)

9. 'Evening Star' (*Death or Glory?*)
10. 'I Want To Be In Love' (*The Dream Society*)
11. 'The Green Man' (*The Green Man*)
12. 'Blackpool' (Edit) (*Sophisticated Beggar*)

From Occident To Orient (2007)
Vinyl Japan label (licensed from Science Friction)
Roy Harper: producer
Peter Richards: producer
Pete Jenner: producer
Roy Harper: vocals, guitar and all songwriting

A Japanese record company negotiated the release of a collectors vinyl album to have for sale on Roy's Japanese tour. It's a rather strange compilation that serves very little purpose. There's nothing new here. It was merely a piece of merchandise but was eventually released in the UK on CD.

1. 'Blackpool' (*Sophisticated Beggar*)
2. 'Francesca' (*Flat Baroque and Berserk*)
3. 'Another Day' (*Flashes from the Archives of Oblivion*)
4. 'Miles Remains' (*Beyond the Door*)
5. 'Wishing Well' (*The Green Man*)
6. 'Frozen Moment' (*Whatever Happened to Jugula?*)
7. 'How Does It Feel' (*Beyond the Door*)
8. 'Pinches Of Salt' (*Garden of Uranium*)
9. 'Elizabeth' (*Whatever Happened to Jugula?*)
10.' Rushing Camelot' (*The Green Man*)
11. 'The Green Man' (*The Green Man*)
12. 'One Of Those Days In England' (*Bullinamingvase*)

Songs Of Love And Loss (2011)
SALVO label
Personnel:
Roy Harper: producer
Peter Richards: producer
Pete Jenner: producer
Roy Harper: vocals, guitar and all songwriting
John Fitzgerald/Roy Harper: remastering
Highest UK chart place: 95

Up to this point, none of Roy's albums had appeared on a digital platform. In 2011, he negotiated a deal with Believe Digital to release nineteen of his albums in batches of four. Part of that deal was for him to create a new compilation of love songs to start the ball rolling.

Roy had already produced one love song compilation – *East Of The Sun* – back in 2001. He'd always intended that to be the first of two; a second one focussing on his laments. This new deal provided the opportunity to revisit that idea.

Disc One
1. 'Black Clouds' (*Sophisticated Beggar*)
2. 'Girlie' (*Sophisticated Beggar*)
3. 'All You Need Is' (*Come Out Fighting Ghengis Smith*)
4.' Francesca' (*Flat Baroque and Berserk*)
5. 'East Of The Sun' (*Flat Baroque and Berserk*)
6. 'Little Lady' (*Lifemask*)
7. 'North Country' (*Valentine*)
8. 'I'll See You Again' (*Valentine*)
9. 'Naked Flame' (*Bullinamingvase*)
10. 'Commune' (*Valentine*)
11. 'Frozen Moment' (*Whatever Happened to Jugula?*)

Disc Two
1. 'Davey' (*Flat Baroque and Berserk*)
2. 'Another Day' (*Flat Baroque and Berserk*)
3. 'South Africa' (*Lifemask*)
4. 'Hallucinating Light' (*HQ*)
5. 'Sleeping At The Wheel' (*Once*)
6. 'Waiting For Godot' (*Death Or Glory?*)
7. 'The Flycatcher' (*Commercial Breaks*)
8. 'On Summer Day' (*Death or Glory?*)
9. 'Cherishing The Lonesome' (*Bullinamingvase*)
10. 'My Friend' (*Sophisticated Beggar*)
11. 'One More Tomorrow' (*Death or Glory?*)
12. 'Forever' (*Valentine*)

Miscellaneous Unreleased Tracks, Guest Appearances and Rarities: 1970-2000

Over the years, there have been songs that were never recorded or were recorded but never considered good enough for release. One unreleased song was performed in a radio session.

Roy recorded a song for Bert Jansch that only featured on his tribute album: *People On The Highway – A Bert Jansch Ecomium*.

He also made a number of guest appearances on friends' albums.

'St Thomas' – The Nice, 1970

This came out of a BBC session. The Nice were going to perform their own version of 'St Thomas', but Roy wrote an impromptu set of words, and they recorded it together on the spot. It's a zany piece of Roy daftness that is quite fun. The track officially surfaced on the 1996 The Nice album, *America – The BBC Sessions*.

'**Ravneferd**' (Lillebjorn Nilsen, Roy Harper)

(On the album *Tilbake* – 1971)

A notable rarity. Lillebjorn is one of Norway's major folk singers. It's an interesting track that starts with the sound of crashing seas, strings and woodwind. Lillebjorn sings in Norwegian with a beautiful clear voice.

The liner notes feature a photo of a poster from a Roy and Lillebjorn concert.

'**Have A Cigar**' – Pink Floyd (Roger Waters), 1975

In 1975, Pink Floyd were recording their follow-up to *Dark Side Of The Moon* – *Wish You Were Here* – at Abbey Road, and Roy was recording *HQ in* the studio next door. Roy and the band had a good rapport. But the Floyd were having trouble getting a vocal for 'Have A Cigar'. They tried Roger, Dave and even a duet of the two but were not happy with the results. Roy cheekily offered to sing it for them in return for a lifetime membership at Lord's Cricket Ground, and they agreed.

The track is a real rock number, based on a churning guitar and bass riff with great drum patterns, additional guitars, synthesizer and electric piano that create a heavy feel. It is Roger Waters' scathing attack on the music business, and Roy's slightly exaggerated performance suits it perfectly.

'**Mr Politician**' – Circa 1982

When touring, The Roy Harper Band played 'Mr Politician' regularly, and it always went down well. It's an irreverent portrayal of politicians, set to a funked-up rhythm, with a rousing chorus: 'Where have all the turkeys gone/ Gone to Westminster every one'. It's one of Roy's piss-take, though not a George Formby.

Roy did record it. The track was laid down in two halves, both of which sounded really good. But for some reason, the two halves were never married together, and it was left off the *Work Of Heart al*bum (probably because it didn't fit the album's ethos).

Presently, the song sits lost and lonely in the archives of oblivion.

'One Man Rock And Roll Band' – Live at Stonehenge (1984)
A CD/DVD of the 1984 Stonehenge Festival – *A Midsummer Night Rock Show* – starts with Roy delivering a blistering version of this, mistakenly titled as 'Rock 'N' Roll Man'.

'Millwall' – Circa 1985
Another song popular at gigs around this time. It's one of Roy's novelty songs. He used to talk in funny voices and ham it up. For the first half, he would wear a fluorescent blue punk Mohican wig and adopt a London accent as a Millwall boot boy. For the second half, he would change the wig to a police helmet but still play the boot boy.

There is a rousing chorus of "'ere we go, 'ere we go, 'ere we go, Millwall'. The song was a lot of fun live but was probably not one that would transfer to vinyl successfully.

'Just A Feeling' – Circa 1989
Roy wrote this just prior to the breaking down of the Berlin Wall and the collapse of the USSR. After playing it for a while at concerts, he tried to record it but wasn't happy with the result. I thought it was a brilliant song. It has such a positive vibe about the changes coming in with the end of the Cold War.

When the Berlin Wall came down on 9 November 1989, I suggested that Roy release the song as a single. It is a serious but catchy number and would've captured the mood of the time perfectly. It's a missing gem.

'Up The 'Pool' (Ian Anderson) (1996)
Roy was asked to contribute to the Jethro Tull tribute, A Collection Of Tull Tales. Tull were massive Roy supporters, but it was very rare for him to cover anyone's work. I know of only three other examples: 'North Country' a traditional; 'Needle Of Death' for the Bert Jansch tribute album; and a verse of Bob Dylan's 'Masters Of War', recorded around 1964/1965 as a contest on Ready Steady Go (probably owned by Dave Clark now), which has never seen the light of day.

For the Tull tribute, Roy chose to sing 'Up the 'Pool'. He delivers this comical Ian Anderson piece in an exaggerated northern accent, describing a day out on the beach at Blackpool: a scene that would've been familiar to both Ian and Roy. Pure 1950s nostalgia. I love that spoken outro, with seagulls and 'Don't forget yer bucket love'.

'Walk With Me' – The Tea Party (1995)
Roy had formed a working relationship with Jeff Martin of Canadian band The
Tea Party. At the end of their album, The Edges Of Twilight, there is a hidden
track on which Roy recites a poem: 'As You Draw Near'.

'Time' – The Tea Party (Alhambra EP 1996)
This was a co-write with The Tea Party's Jeff Martin. Roy takes the vocal on
this six-minute track. It's mainly sung over a rich guitar backing and ends with
Roy's distinctive falsetto.

'Hope' and 'Bad Speech' – Anathema
(From the album Eternity – 1996)
Roy performs the spoken word intro to 'Hope'.

'Needle Of Death' (Bert Jansch) (2000)
Roy was invited to contribute to the 2000 Bert Jansch tribute album, *People On
The Highway – A Bert Jansch Ecomium*. Roy and Bert were old friends from the
Les Cousin days, both having contributed to each others' early albums. 'Needle
Of Death' is a strong song from Bert's self-titled 1965 debut. It was written after
folk singer Buck Polly died from a heroin overdose.

Roy recorded 'Needle Of Death' in his home studio, with The Tea Party's Jeff
Martin, who happened to be staying at the time. The vocal is rich and sad, and
together they produced a masterful interpretation of the Jansch classic.

Roy also made guest appearances on the albums of Dave Gilmour and Kate
Bush.

Dave Gilmour and Roy were good friends and used to hang out together in
the eighties. Indeed, Dave was involved with writing and playing on Roy's 1980
album *The Unknown Soldier*. Roy reciprocated by providing backing vocals
on Dave's second solo album *About Face* in 1983. In 1984 Roy was invited on
stage for a guest appearance at Dave's Hammersmith Odeon concert to sing
Short And Sweet,. This was filmed and Roy's performance was included in
Dave's 1984 Concert video album.

Kate Bush was discovered by Dave Gilmour and was already a Roy Harper
fan. Having duetted with Roy on 'You(The Game Pt.2)' on Roy's *The Unknown
Soldier* album from 1980, Roy reciprocated by providing backing vocals on the
track 'Breathing' on Kate's 1980 *Never For Ever* album. The track was released
as a single and went to number 16 in the UK charts and number 2 in Australia.

Afterword

Over the last few months, I have had the pleasure of playing every single track that Roy has recorded and released, including the official and semi-official live albums. I have also listened to a number of bootleg outtakes that have never seen the light of day. It was quite an undertaking but has been extremely enjoyable. I needed to listen to the songs carefully and repeatedly. Some were brought back to life, and I noticed lyrics and musical segments I had missed in the past.

Roy is now eighty (a miracle to anyone who has known him) and is even writing songs for a new album. He was hoping to have an 80th birthday celebration – another concert at the Royal Festival Hall, but at time of writing, that was on hold.

There's no doubt that during his music career, now spanning 60-years, Roy Harper has produced an amazing number of incredible songs and Roy's legacy is immense.

Left: Roy in mid-flow at the Royal Festival Hall. *(Opher Goodwin)*

Below: Roy looking serious at the Royal Festival Hall in 2016. *(Opher Goodwin)*

Above: A happy Harper performs some skiffle with the magnificent Beth Symonds, who can be seen on double bass in the background. *(Opher Goodwin)*

Below: Backstage at the Royal Festival Hall in 2016. Roy is signing albums for fans. Oke had flown in from Tokyo especially for the gig and was flying straight back in the morning! *(Opher Goodwin)*

Left: A relaxed Roy shares a joke with Bill Shanley as he changes guitars at the Leeds Variety Hall in 2019. *(Opher Goodwin)*

Below: Roy with Bill Shanley next to him during the soundcheck at the Leeds Variety Hall in 2019. *(Opher Goodwin)*

Above: The publicity poster outside the Usher Hall in Edinburgh for Roy's 2016 concert. *(Opher Goodwin)*

Right: The board outside the DeBarras Folk Club in Clonakilty in 2013. *(Steve Tomalin)*

On Track series

Barclay James Harvest – Keith and Monica Domone 978-1-78952-067-5
The Beatles – Andrew Wild 978-1-78952-009-5
The Beatles Solo 1969-1980 – Andrew Wild 978-1-78952-030-9
Blue Oyster Cult – Jacob Holm-Lupo 978-1-78952-007-1
Kate Bush – Bill Thomas 978-1-78952-097-2
The Clash – Nick Assirati 978-1-78952-077-4
Crosby, Stills and Nash – Andrew Wild 978-1-78952-039-2
Deep Purple and Rainbow 1968-79 – Steve Pilkington 978-1-78952-002-6
Dire Straits – Andrew Wild 978-1-78952-044-6
Dream Theater – Jordan Blum 978-1-78952-050-7
Emerson Lake and Palmer – Mike Goode 978-1-78952-000-2
Fairport Convention – Kevan Furbank 978-1-78952-051-4
Genesis – Stuart MacFarlane 978-1-78952-005-7
Gentle Giant – Gary Steel 978-1-78952-058-3
Hawkwind – Duncan Harris 978-1-78952-052-1
Iron Maiden – Steve Pilkington 978-1-78952-061-3
Jethro Tull – Jordan Blum 978-1-78952-016-3
Elton John in the 1970s – Peter Kearns 978-1-78952-034-7
Gong – Kevan Furbank 978-1-78952-082-8
Iron Maiden – Steve Pilkington 978-1-78952-061-3
Judas Priest – John Tucker 978-1-78952-018-7
Kansas – Kevin Cummings 978-1-78952-057-6
Aimee Mann – Jez Rowden 978-1-78952-036-1
Joni Mitchell – Peter Kearns 978-1-78952-081-1
The Moody Blues – Geoffrey Feakes 978-1-78952-042-2
Mike Oldfield – Ryan Yard 978-1-78952-060-6
Queen – Andrew Wild 978-1-78952-003-3
Renaissance – David Detmer 978-1-78952-062-0
The Rolling Stones 1963-80 – Steve Pilkington 978-1-78952-017-0
Steely Dan – Jez Rowden 978-1-78952-043-9
Thin Lizzy – Graeme Stroud 978-1-78952-064-4
Toto – Jacob Holm-Lupo 978-1-78952-019-4
U2 – Eoghan Lyng 978-1-78952-078-1
UFO – Richard James 978-1-78952-073-6
The Who – Geoffrey Feakes 978-1-78952-076-7
Roy Wood and the Move – James R Turner 978-1-78952-008-8
Van Der Graaf Generator – Dan Coffey 978-1-78952-031-6
Yes – Stephen Lambe 978-1-78952-001-9
Frank Zappa 1966 to 1979 – Eric Benac 978-1-78952-033-0
10CC – Peter Kearns 978-1-78952-054-5

and many more to come!

Would you like to write for Sonicbond Publishing?

We are mainly a music publisher, but we also occasionally publish in other genres including film and television. At Sonicbond Publishing we are always on the look-out for authors, particularly for our two main series, On Track and Decades.

Mixing fact with in depth analysis, the On Track series examines the entire recorded work of a particular musical artist or group. All genres are considered from easy listening and jazz to 60s soul to 90s pop, via rock and metal.

The Decades series singles out a particular decade in an artist or group's history and focuses on that decade in more detail than may be allowed in the On Track series.

While professional writing experience would, of course, be an advantage, the most important qualification is to have real enthusiasm and knowledge of your subject. First-time authors are welcomed, but the ability to write well in English is essential.

Sonicbond Publishing has distribution throughout Europe and North America, and all our books are also published in E-book form. Authors will be paid a royalty based on sales of their book. Further details about our books are available from www.sonicbondpublishing.com. To contact us, complete the contact form there or email info@sonicbondpublishing.co.uk